D0903944

ONE HUNDRED AND ONE YEARS OF

HOCKEY

The Chronicle of a Century on Ice

ONE HUNDRED AND ONE YEARS OF

HOCKEY

The Chronicle of a Century on Ice

EDITED BY AL STRACHAN

Written by Eric Duhatschek • Red Fisher • Trent Frayne •

Al Strachan • Rejean Tremblay

KEY PORTER ✒ BOOKS

Copyright © 1999, 2000 by Key Porter Books

All rights reserved. No part of this work covered by the copyrights hereon may be reproduced or used in any form or by any means—graphic, electronic or mechanical, including photocopying, recording, taping or information storage and retrieval systems—without the prior written permission of the publisher, or in the case of photocopying or other reprographic copying, a license from the Canadian Copyright Licensing Agency.

Canadian Cataloguing in Publication Data

Main entry under title:

101 years of hockey

ISBN 1-55263-314-4

1. Hockey – History.   2. National Hockey League – History.   I. Strachan, Al
II. Title: One hundred years of hockey.

GV846.5.053 1999   796.962'09   C99-931095-X

The Canada Council | Le Conseil des Arts
FOR THE ARTS | DU CANADA
SINCE 1957 | DEPUIS 1957

The publisher gratefully acknowledges the support of the Canada Council for the Arts and the Ontario Arts Council for its publishing program.

Canadä

We acknowledge the financial support of the Government of Canada through the Book Publishing Industry Development Program (BPIDP) for our publishing activities.

Key Porter Books Limited
70 The Esplanade
Toronto, Ontario
Canada M5E 1R2

www.keyporter.com

Typeset in Today Sans Serif and Minion
Electronic formatting: Heidi Palfrey
Design: Peter Maher

Printed and bound in Spain

00 01 02 03 6 5 4 3 2

CONTENTS

Introduction by Al Strachan / 9

The Early Years Trent Frayne / 10

The Original Six Red Fisher / 36

The Expansion Era Rejean Tremblay / 84

The Dynasties *Al Strachan* / 138

The Modern Game *Eric Duhatschek* / 194

Farewell to a Legend / 282

1999-2000 Playoffs / 290

For those of use who love hockey—and our numbers are rapidly increasing, not only in North America, but in Europe and even Asia—no other game can match it.

It is game of artistry and grace, but it can also be powerful and even violent. It has finesse and creativity, but it also has the brute force of heavy hitting and blistering slapshots. The game's history is just as varied. Some teams can reflect on glory and dynasties while others have little to show but futility. Others simply ceased to exist.

In *One Hundred Years of Hockey* we've tried to provide an insightful overview of North American hockey, charting its changes as it developed over the course of the twentieth century.

Five hockey writers who have themselves spent more than a century covering the game bring to life some of the early characters who dominated the professional leagues, even before the NHL emerged as the acknowledged upper echelon. The great stars of the later eras, Gordie Howe, Maurice Richard, Bobby Orr, Wayne Gretzky, Mario Lemieux, and so many others are also profiled.

There are also the stories behind the powerful dynasties that dominated the sport for so many years, from the Montreal Canadiens to the Toronto Maple Leafs, to the Canadiens again and then on to the New York Islanders and Edmonton Oilers.

By the '90s, the dynasties were gone, perhaps a function of the changing economics, but the NHL had emerged into the entity we now know so well—essentially a world all-star league.

The qualifications for participation in the National Hockey League are simple. If you're the best in the world, you're welcome. If there's someone better, you're gone.

No book could ever be as rewarding as the game itself. But if your knowledge and enjoyment of that great game is increased even a little bit, then we have been successful in our endeavor.

AL STRACHAN

By the time the third millennium began, the most famous sports trophy in the world was 108 years old, the creation of a foreign diplomat who watched two of his sons chase a hockey puck across the frozen waters of Ottawa's Rideau Canal in the dead of winter.

This, at any rate, is one version of how Lord Stanley of Preston, the governor general of Canada near the end of the 19th century, was inspired to create the trophy that bears his name and nowadays is the tallest prize a professional hockey team can win. His lordship, an Englishman whose favorite game was cricket, spent 10 guineas, about $48.60, to have the trophy made by a British silversmith. It was a dumpy bowl, seven-and-a-half inches high and just under 12 inches across, and according to D'Arcy Jenish in his 1992 book, *The Stanley Cup*, it looked like a soup tureen.

There are other versions of how Lord Stanley was moved to establish this coveted award. Every winter, as hockey fervor grew across the country, he instructed his staff to freeze an outdoor rink on the grounds at Rideau Hall, the governor general's residence. There, two of his lordship's eight sons, Arthur and Edward, played against local Ottawa teams. Aware of the game's growing popularity, his lordship instructed an aide to deliver a message to a roomful of hockey players at a downtown banquet.

"I have for some time been thinking," read the aide, quoting the governor general, "that it would be a good thing if there were a challenge cup which would be held from year to year by the leading hockey club in Canada. I am willing to give a cup that shall be held annually by the winning club."

Lord Stanley, a modest man, planned to call

his trophy the Dominion Hockey Challenge Cup, but the heavy-handed title didn't last; by 1893, when the Montreal Amateur Athletic Association became the trophy's first winner, everyone was calling it the Stanley Cup. As scriptwriter Andrew Gardner noted in *Legends of Hockey*, Derik Murray's affectionate five-part 1996 television documentary, "This country, in the sense of nationhood, would be forged from Lord Stanley's simple idea."

Back then, any team could play for the trophy by sending a challenge to a pair of trustees appointed by Lord Stanley. This panel decided who would play the Cup holders. Challenges were numerous: 54 challenges and 132 games had been played by 1927, when the National Hockey League became sole owner of the Stanley Cup and made the trophy its very own.

Of all the challenges in that early period, none was more unexpected than one late in 1904 from Dawson City in the far reaches of Canada's Northwest, a saga as bizarre today as it was nearly a century ago. This team, the Nuggets, playing in the shadow of the Arctic Circle, was the creation of a Toronto-born prospector, Joe Boyle, who had struck it rich in the Yukon gold rush of 1898. Boyle was a flamboyant adventurer who, before cashing in his chips a quarter-century after his huge strike, travelled to Russia to fight the Bolsheviks during the Russian Revolution.

Left: Lord Stanley of Preston was governor general of Canada when he donated the cup that eventually bore his name.

Above: The original Stanley Cup was small by today's standards. It has grown over the years as sequences of bands have been added to provide room for inscriptions of Cup-winning teams and players.

Right: Nowadays it's often called the battered old mug.

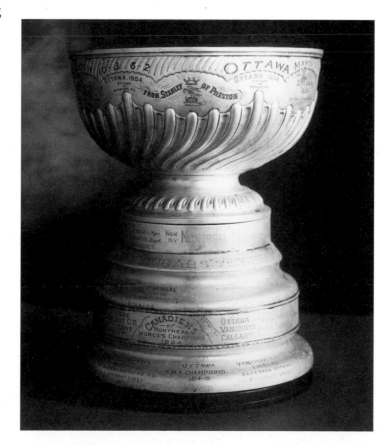

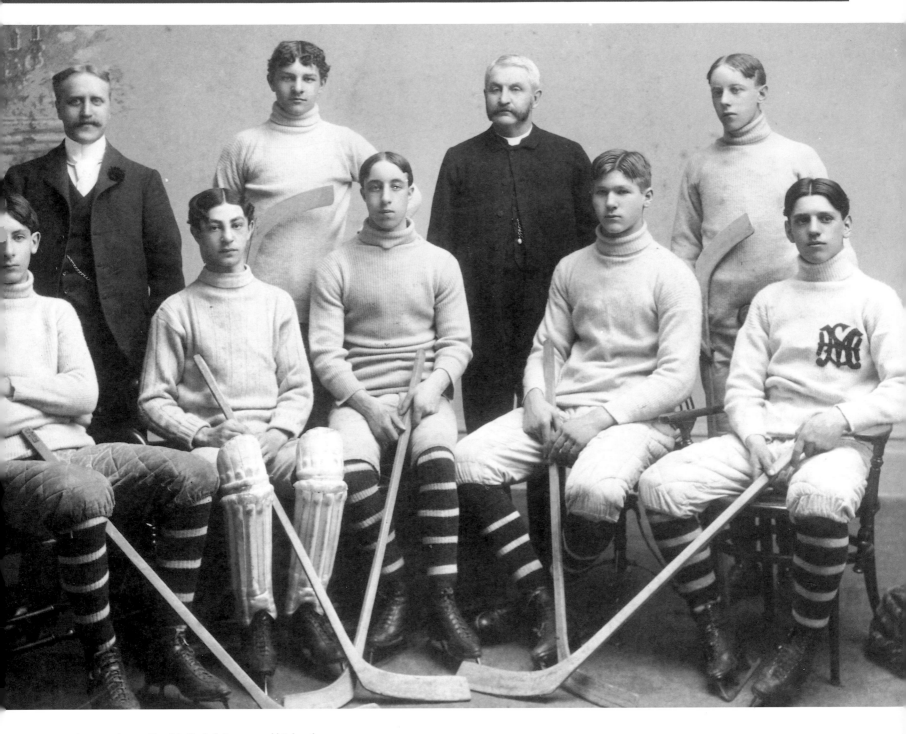

A young Lester Patrick, far left. Lester and his brother
Frank were two of the most influential builders of
professional hockey as players, coaches, general managers,
and even owners.

Boyle was a persuasive guy. He induced the Nugget players to join in the wacky scheme, which required them to travel 4,000 miles to play against Ottawa's renowned Silver Seven. The high cost of the journey—almost $3,000—was raised in part by the Nuggets themselves, who sponsored dances and sold raffle tickets. Then, on December 19, 1904, they set off for Ottawa on dog sleighs and even bicycles. Storms and high winds forced them to walk most of the 320 miles to Whitehorse, which they reached in 13 days.

At Whitehorse they boarded a train to Skagway, Alaska, the port from which the boat to Vancouver sailed. They arrived at Skagway to learn that the ship had sailed two hours earlier, and had to spend five aimless days waiting for the next ship south. From Vancouver they boarded a train for a tedious ride eastward through the mountains, across the frozen Prairies, and over the snowbound rock of Lake Superior's north shore. At last, 23 weary days later, on January 11, 1905, they arrived in Ottawa.

Unfortunately for the Dawson tourists, having reached Ottawa they ran into Frank McGee of Ottawa's Silver Seven, the greatest goal scorer of his day. Although blind in one eye, McGee was so good that even before his death he was referred to as "the legendary Frank McGee." In two games the visitors from the Klondike lost 9–2 and 23–2. In that second game McGee scored fourteen goals, four of them in 140 seconds.

Frank often collected goals in bunches. Once, playing the Silver Seven's most persistent rival, the Montreal Wanderers, he scored eight. In eight Stanley Cup games in 1904 he scored 21 goals, and a year later he scored 18 goals in four games.

In 1914, at age 35 and retired from hockey, Frank volunteered for overseas service in World War I. In spite of his sightless eye, he was accepted. He was wounded in France in December 1915 and spent nine months recovering in England. D'Arcy Jenish writes in *The Stanley Cup* that on September 4, 1916, Frank wrote a letter to his brother, D'Arcy McGee, an Ottawa lawyer, saying that he had been offered a posting in Le Havre, well behind the front lines. Instead he returned to combat. Twelve days later the great Frank McGee was killed in action.

A star at almost every sport, Lionel Conacher was voted Canada's athlete of the half-century in 1950. In hockey he was a bod-thumping defenseman and fearless shot-blocker who defended for two Stanley Cup winners, the Chicago Blackhawks and the Montreal Maroons. He was a good coach, too.

At home, the year 1916 saw significant developments. The Montreal Canadiens, who would win the Stanley Cup 24 times before the end of the century, took home Lord Stanley's trophy for the first time. Their victim was the first American entry to appear in the Cup final, the Portland Rosebuds, an Oregon entrant that was about as American as Pierre Elliott Trudeau.

This contradiction can be traced to two families—the Patrick brothers, Lester and Frank, and the O'Briens, father and son, Michael J. and J. Ambrose. Without the Patricks there would have been no Portland Rosebuds (or Pacific Coast Hockey Association, either), and without the O'Briens there would have been no Montreal Canadiens (or National Hockey Association, the forerunner of the National Hockey League).

The Patricks are surely the world's most remarkable hockey family. For 40 years Lester or Frank (and sometimes both) dominated in the game, and for almost the entire century there has been a Patrick somewhere in the game's major leagues.

Lester's sons, Lynn and Muzz, were regulars with the New York Rangers in the 1940s, and helped them win the Stanley Cup in 1940. In the 1950s both became coaches and general managers, of the Boston Bruins and the Rangers, respectively. When the NHL expanded in 1967, Lynn was hired as the senior vice president of the St. Louis Blues. His cousin, Dick Patrick, has been an executive with the Washington Capitals since 1982. Craig Patrick, Lynn's son, spent seven seasons as an NHL player beginning in 1971, then became the youngest general manager in New York Rangers history in 1980. In 1989, he was hired as

general manager of the Pittsburgh Penguins. He was there to greet the new millennium, thus completing nearly a century of Patricks—a century that can be traced back to the day in 1904 when his grandfather Lester, at the age of 20, joined the Brandon Wheat Kings for an unsuccessful challenge to the Ottawa Silver Seven for the Stanley Cup.

Frank and Lester were the kingpins of the family. Early in their careers they made good money playing in Eastern

Above left: Frank Patrick at 28. He went west to the Pacific Coast to join brother Lester and introduce the pro game there.

Left: Frank, the handsome entrepreneur.

Right: Before backup goaltenders, regular players sometimes replaced injured goalers. In a rare incident Lester Patrick, coach of the New York Rangers, once replaced Lorne Chabot in the Stanley Cup final. He won, too.

Canada. Then, in 1911, they moved to the West Coast, where they organized and ran their own league, built and owned their own rinks, raided rival leagues to sign players, made up their own rules, and owned, managed, coached, and played on their own teams.

Because of Lester's later prominence with the New York Rangers (over 20 years as coach, then general manager, then vice president of hockey at Madison Square Garden), he is perhaps better remembered than his brother. But Frank made huge contributions to the game's evolution. He "invented" artificial-ice rinks, post-season playoffs, and the system under which the Stanley Cup final is played today. He introduced the penalty shot, the forward pass, and assists for players helping on a goal, and he legalized kicking the puck. He even invented the game's blue lines.

In many ways the Patrick brothers were dissimilar. Frank was a risk-taker and an outgoing, enthusiastic salesman. Lester was the practical, conservative one, and a tireless though somewhat tedious talker. Frank was a big drinker and a party guy; Lester was wary of booze.

Their father, Joseph Patrick, was in the lumber business in Drummondville, Quebec. Later he moved his wife and eight children to the lush forests of interior British Columbia. By 1911, a wealthy man, he had brought his family to Vancouver. There, Frank and Lester, who had been playing pro hockey in eastern Canada, encountered many people who lamented that they had never seen a game. That intrigued Frank.

"Why not," he is reported to have said to his father and Lester, "why not build a couple of rinks out here and start a hockey league?"

Joseph liked the idea. Lester, cautious as usual, demurred. He was persuaded when Frank said he'd heard of a business in the East that manufactured a machine that could freeze water indoors and keep it frozen.

The Patricks launched plans to build a $350,000, 10,000 seat arena in Vancouver and a smaller arena in Victoria. Frank designed the buildings and supervised construction at both locations. They were the first artificial-ice rinks in Canada. Lester went East to arrange for delivery of the ice machines and, on the side, lined up good hockey players.

The earnest-talking Lester managed to steal Cyclone Taylor and Newsy Lalonde, two of the biggest names in eastern hockey.

Back in British Columbia, Lester took charge of the Victoria Aristocrats as player, coach, manager, and co-owner. Frank, the league president, did likewise for the Vancouver Millionaires. Then the Patricks must have run out of brothers. They hired an outsider, Jimmy Gardner, to run the third team, the New Westminster Royals.

When interest in hockey expanded across the border into Oregon, the flamboyant Frank Patrick met with businessmen there and promised that he would supply players if they built a rink. When they did, he did. He transferred his New Westminster franchise to Portland and named the team, oddly, the Rosebuds. In this manner, hockey was introduced to the United States. The first puck dropped there on December 8, 1914.

A year later, the Rosebuds were in Montreal to battle a new entrant for the Stanley Cup: an assortment of French-Canadian players who called themselves the Montreal Canadiens. The team was founded by the aforementioned J. Ambrose O'Brien. It happened that in 1909 O'Brien's wealthy father, Michael J. O'Brien, decided he wanted an Eastern Canada Hockey Association team in his hometown of Renfrew, Ontario. The

Newsy Lalonde

The Renfrew Millionaires

senior O'Brien, whose fortune came from railways and one of Northern Ontario's richest silver mines, had little interest in hockey, but he recognized that the burgeoning sport was a good investment. He therefore was outraged when his application for admission into the league was rejected—twice.

His independent Renfrew team, mysteriously called the Creamery Kings, were anything but milk cans. Lester Patrick had signed for an enormous sum—$3,000 for a 12-game season—on the condition that his brother Frank also be signed—for $2,000. So both O'Briens fumed at the rejections. Then Ambrose remembered a conversation he'd had with

James Strachan, manager of the Montreal Wanderers, who observed that a team made up mostly of French Canadians would attract a huge following among the 70 percent of Montreal's population who were French.

So on December 4th, 1909, Michael J. O'Brien financed a team he called Les Canadiens and deposited $5,000 in a St. James Street bank to guarantee the players' salaries.

To round out a four-team league, Ambrose O'Brien persuaded Strachan to transfer his Montreal Wanderers to the newly created National Hockey Association, made up of Renfrew, Cobalt, and Haileybury in the booming mining belt of Northern Ontario. By 1916 the stage was set for a Stanley Cup final between the American invader, the Portland Rosebuds, all of whom were Canadians, and the Flying Frenchmen of Quebec, their roster full of names like Jack Laviolette, Louis Berlinguette, Didier Pitre, Georges Poulin, Jacques Fournier, and a goaltender whose name will live forever— or at least as long as there is a Georges Vezina Trophy, awarded every year to the NHL's best goaltender.

Georges was a remarkable fellow, not least because he sired 22 children—three sets of triplets and 13 single births—and died at age 39. He was a busy man in other ways. In 15 seasons with the Canadiens, Georges never missed a game—a streak that

The Vezina Trophy, awarded annually to the NHL's top goaltender, is named for Georges Vezina, who spent 15 seasons in goal for the Montreal Canadiens. He died of tuberculosis in 1926, four months after he collapsed in front of the net.

Frank Nighbor, a poke-checking wizard, inspired Lady Byng to donate the trophy that bears her name. It goes to the NHL's most sportsmanlike player.

included 328 league games and 39 in the playoffs (which included winning Stanley Cup finals in 1924). On the ice he was imperturbable, cool as a cucumber. Since he came from Chicoutimi, he became known as the Chicoutimi Cucumber.

The Canadiens had been lucky to acquire him. They were on an exhibition tour of French-speaking townships east of Montreal when they fetched up in Chicoutimi, a lumber town on the Saguenay River, to play the local rubes. Rubes indeed! The vaunted Habitants could not get the puck past a tall, calm, lanky kid of 23 playing in goal for the locals. Vezina, of course. They signed him without delay.

Vezina never learned English, so his quotes in that language are nonexistent. But he needed no English to play goal, and he wore the famed *bleu, blanc, et rouge* from the moment of his debut in 1910 until a game on November 28, 1925, in Pittsburgh, when he was playing with chest pains and a fever of 103. In the dressing room after the first period he suffered a slight hemorrhage, but he returned to play. Suddenly he dropped to the ice in front of his net. Teammates carried him off, and the diagnosis was tuberculosis.

Back in Montreal, Georges made one last, poignant trip to the Canadiens' dressing room. He wanted his hockey sweater. He died on March 26, 1926, in Chicoutimi, only four months after his final game.

Vezina was present in 1919 when the Canadiens played the Stanley Cup final in Seattle against Frank Patrick's Metropolitans. Patrick was president of the league that Seattle represented. It was the year of a worldwide influenza epidemic, and wary hockey fans wore gauze masks at the Stanley Cup games. All but three Canadiens players came down with the flu, the most seriously ill of them being Bad Joe Hall, a player renowned for carving the faces and anatomy of opposing hockey players with his stick.

In the fifth game, Hall was desperately ill, worn down by his exertions in the fourth game, which went 40 minutes of overtime and ended with the score 0–0. Vezina seemed to onlookers to be deflecting pucks with the grace and insouciance of a symphony conductor. However, with the teams tied at two games and a tie, so many players were ill or bedridden that for the only time in Stanley Cup history the series was abandoned. It was too late for Joe Hall. He was taken to a Seattle hospital, where he died six days later.

One reason that Vezina played on only two Stanley Cup winners in his 15 seasons was Frank Nighbor, a tall, handsome star center for the Ottawa Senators. In 1920, '21 and '23, the Senators, spearheaded by Nighbor, beat off the Canadiens in the East and went on to win the Stanley Cup.

Nighbor was a poke-checking wizard, so good with an oversized stick that rival teams claimed the Ottawa playing surface had been shaped to edge opposing puck carriers toward center ice where Nighbor could more easily get at them. Frank could score, too. From 1915 to 1930 he was a 60-minute man with such dignity and power that Lady Byng, wife of the governor general of the time, donated a trophy to the league as a reward for the NHL's most gentlemanly skilled player. Nighbor won the Lady Byng Trophy the first two years it was offered, 1925 and 1926. Also, in 1924 he was the first winner of the Hart Trophy, the top award for a hockey player in the NHL. As they say on squawk radio, Frank came to play.

So did another Ottawa alumnus, Fred (Cyclone) Taylor. He was born in Tara, Ontario, on June 23, 1883, and raised in Listowel, Ontario, where the town barber gave him his first pair of skates. During the Nickel Belt player raids of the early 1900s, the dashing Taylor

Fred (Cyclone) Taylor was a dominant player. He starred with the Ottawa Senators before moving to Vancouver to play for his former teammates, Lester and Frank Patrick.

demanded and got an unheard-of salary of $5,250 to jump from the Senators to the newly hatched Renfrew Millionaires.

Taylor, whose whirlwind style inspired the governor general, Earl Grey, to call him Cyclone, was with the Senators in 1909 at a salary of $2,800, which he augmented with a $35-a-month job as a clerk in the federal immigration department. Then along came Renfrew. Frank Cosentino in his 1990 book *The Renfrew Millionaires* called Taylor the highest-paid athlete in the world at that time, on a per game basis. "He was being paid $5,250 for a 12-game season over two months. Ty Cobb, the great American baseball player, had recently signed for $6,500. That was over seven months and 154 games."

Taylor could skate a hole in the wind. Once, playing against the Montreal Shamrocks, he carried the puck end to end, zipping at top speed around the opposing net. Suddenly, though untouched, he crashed into the boards. He was carried to the dressing room, where a doctor cut off one of his skates and found the boot soaked in blood from a deep, 3-inch slice in his foot. Cyclone had been traveling at such speed as he banked around the net that his own left skate had cut through his right boot and ripped the foot.

In 1912, Cyclone went to Vancouver to join the Patrick brothers, with whom he had played in Renfrew. He took with him the legend that one night in the East, skating backwards, he had carried the puck the length of the ice past rival players and scored on a bedazzled goaltender. Did it really happen? Until Cyclone's dying day—June 9, 1979, just two weeks before his ninety-sixth birthday—he'd get a twinkle in his eye when asked to confirm or deny, and he'd say, "Well now, I don't want to spoil someone's story." And that would be it.

But some 40 years after Taylor's move west, the noted historian Bruce Hutchison wrote a piece in *Maclean's* magazine after a long interview with Lester Patrick, who presented another version of Cyclone's fabled feat. Patrick debunked it.

"On one of his rushes the Ottawa defense stopped him cold and turned him around with his back to the Ottawa goal," Patrick told Hutchison. "He flipped the puck, back-handed. It nosed past the goal-

tender. I was on the ice and saw the whole thing and we went on playing. But by the time the sports writers had finished with it, you'd have thought the Cyclone repeated this performance just about every night afterwards."

In the years following his retirement, Taylor was often pleased when the dashing skating style of a new meteor with the Montreal Canadiens was compared to his own. This was the explosive Howie Morenz, center on a high-scoring line with Johnny (Black Cat) Gagnon and Aurel Joliat. For a dozen years beginning in the early 1920s, Morenz was the biggest star in hockey, often referred to in such outposts as New York, Boston, and Chicago as "the Babe Ruth of hockey."

Morenz had a blocky build and a powerful stride with instant acceleration. He could be knocked down, but he wouldn't stay down. He'd bounce to his feet, yell for the puck, and set off on another twisting drive toward the enemy net. In 1950 he was voted Canada's outstanding hockey player of the half-century.

Left: Aurel Joliat stares sadly at the equipment of former linemate Morenz in the first game following Howie's death.

Right: Morenz was a dashing figure for *les Canadiens,* the finest player of his time. His sweater number was 7 but the little goaltender for the New York Americans, Roy Worters, said that when Howie wound up behind the Montreal net for a dash down the ice, "He was wearing No. 777!"

In 1937 NHL all-stars played a benefit game for the widow and family of Howie Morenz, the dazzling Canadien star who died early that year after a broken leg ended his hockey career.

In his great days with the Canadiens, Morenz was almost impossible to stop. Lester Patrick thought he had the answer in the Stanley Cup final of 1925 when the defending Cup holders went west to engage Lester's Victoria Cougars (Lester dropped the original name, the Aristocrats). Patrick instructed his versatile 29-year-old center, Frank Fredrickson, to hound Morenz every move he made. Fredrickson had long been a star, an eye-catching player with his tall, lean build—an all elbows-and-knees kind of frame—and his long-striding skating style.

Indeed, he did stalk Morenz as the Cougars went to work on the visiting Habitants. They won the opening game 5–2 and the second 3–1, with Morenz and his famous No. 7 rarely able to shake Fredrickson. But in the third game, with the possibility looming of a humiliating sweep, Morenz broke loose from his nemesis and scored a three-goal hat trick. The Canadiens won 4–2 and prolonged the series.

Fredrickson was far too experienced to regard Howie's outburst as more than a temporary fluke. Back went the blanket in Game 4 as Morenz tired in the 60-minute ordeal (it was still an era of 60-minute men, with substitutes allowed only when a regular was injured). The Cougars won the Stanley Cup with a 6–1 clincher.

In the Fall of 1934 Morenz was traded to Chicago by the Canadiens' owner Leo Dandurand, who claimed that he did it to spare the fading star the boos of the Montreal Forum zealots. Morenz played fitfully in Chicago and was traded to the New York Rangers. In 1936, Cecil Hart, Morenz's coach for 6 years in Montreal, returned to the Canadiens. One of his first moves was to acquire Morenz and reunite him with Joliat and Gagnon. Soon Morenz was Howie the Howitzer again, or close to it.

But he soon met a tragic end. One night in January 1937, he was checked by Chicago defenseman Earl Seibert and caught his skate in the Forum boards. His left leg twisted under him, breaking three bones in the ankle and one in the leg. Morenz was 34, and he recognized as he lay in hospital that his hockey career might be over. He grew agitated, and one night, six weeks after the break, he lurched from his bed, dragging the leg in its heavy cast. He crashed to the floor, struggled to his feet, then collapsed, dead. The death certificate gave the cause as "cardiac deficiency and acute excitement." What some people called it was a broken heart.

Fredrickson enjoyed an intriguing career both before and after the Morenz episode. He was a Winnipeg-born Icelander, the captain of the city's Falcons, Canada's Gold Medal winners in the 1920 Olympics. During World War I he became a Royal Flying Corps pilot, and in 1918, while returning to England from Egypt, his ship was torpedoed and sunk by a German submarine. A Japanese ship rescued him from the Atlantic.

Fredrickson was an accomplished violinist. After the war he played with the dance band in Winnipeg's Fort Garry Hotel. It was there that Lester Patrick caught up with him and offered him $4,000 to turn pro with the Victoria Cougars. Later, Frank played in the NHL with Detroit and Boston. Then he coached the Pittsburgh Pirates in their 1929–30

Frank Fredrickson was an accomplished defensive player who, in a Stanley Cup final of 1924–25, drew the role of checking the great Morenz. He did, too, as the Victoria Cougars triumphed 3 games to 1.

Opposite: Jacques Plante popularized the goaltender's mask but it was Clint Benedict who first wore one in a game–some 30 years before Plante covered up.

season before going on to coach hockey at Princeton University in New Jersey. There, he could sometimes be found in the company of another violinist, a mathematics professor named Albert Einstein. Sportswriter Jim Coleman once quipped that Frank quit Princeton because Einstein refused to play a violin duet with him.

Fredrickson's exposure to the NHL was occasioned by the collapse of the Western Canada Hockey League in 1925. A year earlier, the Patrick brothers' Pacific Coast League had folded when the Seattle Metropolitans went under. So the Patricks' teams in Victoria and Vancouver joined Edmonton, Calgary, Saskatoon, and Regina in the Western Canada League. It collapsed following the Stanley Cup series of 1926 when the Montreal Maroons, with goaltender Clint Benedict racking up three shutouts, beat Fredrickson's Cougars three games to one. It was the last time the two leagues, East and West, would play for the Cup.

It was also the final Cup appearance for Clint Benedict, who predated Jacques Plante by close to 30 years in experimenting with a goaltender's face mask. Benedict, who backstopped four winning Stanley Cup teams and two defeated finalists, was called the Praying Netminder because of the trick he had of dropping to his knees to smother pucks. This was in the era when goaltenders were not permitted to leave their feet. Because of him, the rule was changed to permit flopping.

Once, dropping down, Clint caught a blast from Howie Morenz directly on a leather mask he was trying out. The puck slashed open his forehead and broke his nose, injuries which sidelined him for seven weeks. That happened during the 1930–31 season, Clint's final one in the NHL and his seventeenth as a pro. But he was a bear for punishment. The following year he went to a team in the old International-American Hockey League for one more season. Then, at 36, he hung up his gear for good.

By that time there were only two Canadian towns left in professional hockey—Montreal and Toronto. Since 1924, when the Boston Bruins became the league's first American team, the NHL had expanded to 10 teams. Most Canadian towns could no longer compete financially with big cities like New York, Pittsburgh, Philadelphia, and Chicago. When

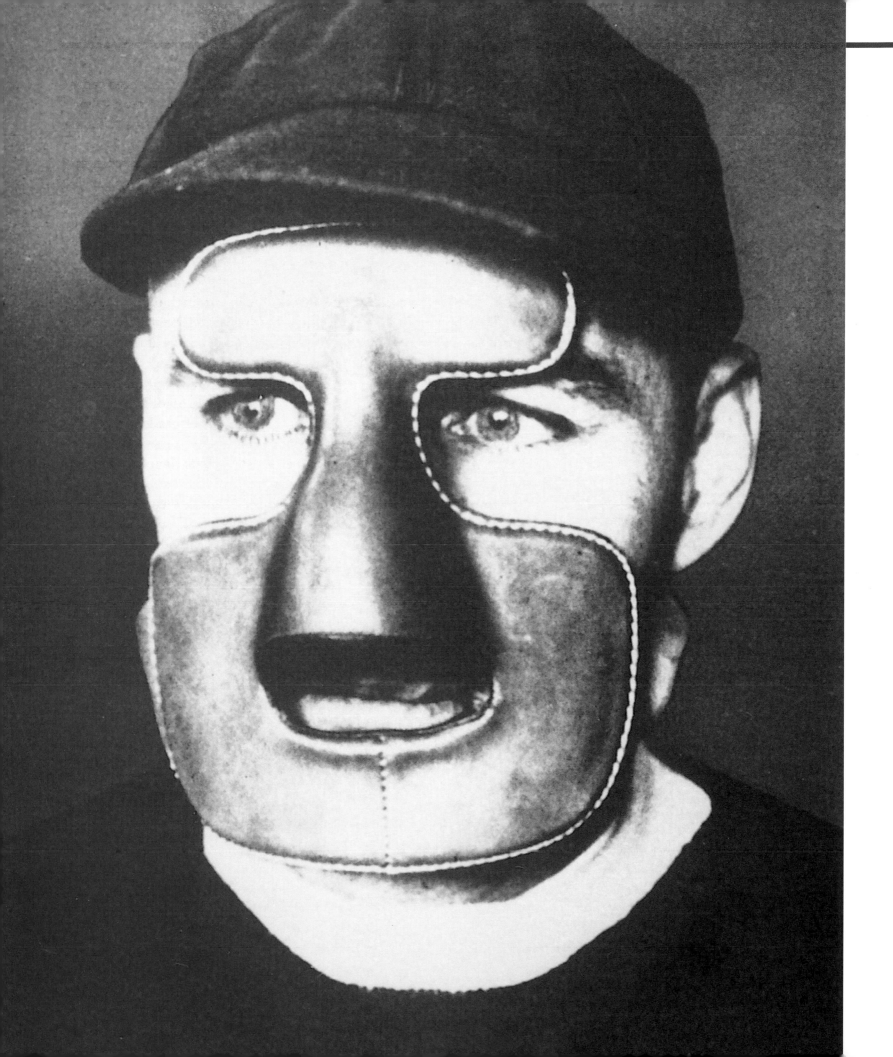

Hooley Smith, who became a star with the old Montreal Maroons, was one of Canada's brightest lights at the 1924 Olympic Games in Chamonix, France.

the Edmonton Eskimos went down, the Edmonton Journal noted sadly the enormous disparity between the old-time cities and the new: "New York pro hockey outdrew the combined attendance of any four cities in the Western league."

Players from the West helped fill the rosters of the NHL newcomers. Elsewhere, Canada's dominance of the game soared. Beginning with Fredrickson's Winnipeg Falcons in 1920, Canadian teams won four straight Olympic gold medals, and some of their victories were mind-blowers. In that 1920 appearance at the Summer Olympics in Antwerp, the Canadians hammered Czechoslovakia 15–0, and Sweden 12–1. Perhaps exhausted, they eked out a mere 2–0 win over the United States in the semifinal before beating Sweden 12–1 in the final game.

Antwerp was the only time hockey was conducted at the Summer Olympics. Officials in the host city had decided to augment the summer program with figure-skating, speed-skating, and ice hockey. They forwarded an invitation to the Canadian Amateur Hockey Association, whose officials had no idea which team to send overseas. It happened that the Winnipeg Falcons were in the East, where they had beaten Toronto's Eastern champions in the national senior final, so it was decided to send them. The Falcons weren't even given time to return to Winnipeg to pack their bags for Europe. They were put on a train for Saint John, New Brunswick, to board *S.S. Mekita* for the Atlantic crossing. The CAHA gave each player $25 expenses "to purchase haberdashery."

Canada's next Olympic foray was in 1924 on an open-air rink in Chamonix, France. That year, the Toronto Granites were even more overwhelming than the Falcons. In the preliminary round of the eight-team tournament, with future NHL stars Dunc Munro and Hooley Smith leading the assault, the Granites demolished teams from three countries by a combined 85–0. They hammered the Czechs 30–0, the Swedes 22–0, and the Swiss 33–0. In the semifinal the Canadians kayoed Great Britain 19–2. Then they handled the troublesome Americans 6–1 in the gold medal game.

At one point during the Chamonix assault, Dunc Munro turned to his own goal and was startled, since play was in progress, to find it empty. Glancing about, he spotted the goaltender, Jack Cameron, chatting up a pair of young women at rinkside. A nice way to score a shutout, he recalled.

In 1928 at St. Moritz, the Varsity Grads, made up mostly of former students at the University of Toronto, had an equally soft time winning the gold medal—a task made simpler by the absence of a team from the United States. The Grads beat Sweden 11–0, Britain 14–0, and Switzerland 13–0. These easy victories may have led Canadians to become overconfident. In 1932 a team from Winnipeg, imaginatively calling itself the Winnipegs, met an American team at Lake Placid in upstate New York. In the first game of the double round robin the pesky Americans held the Canadians to a mere 2–1 overtime win. When the teams met again in the second round, the Americans led 2–1 with less than a minute to play.

Sportswriter Jim Coleman, who was there, reports that when Winnipeg's defenseman Hack Simpson dawdled with the puck, the coach Jack Hughes shouted in anguish, "Move it! There's only 35 seconds left!" Simpson replied amiably, "That's lots of time."

Simpson then passed the puck to left winger Romeo Rivers, who scored to send the game into overtime. After three periods of scoreless overtime, the Canadians were awarded the Gold Medal on the grounds that the Americans had been unable to beat them in two games.

In the 1936 Olympic record book, there appears to be a misprint: the gold medalist is listed as Great Britain. It's all too true. Canada's entry was outmaneuvered by a wily fellow named J.F. (Bunny) Ahearne, the general secretary of the British Hockey Association. Ahearne had a spy in the CAHA registry office in Canada who made a list of registered players born in Great Britain to parents who later migrated to Canada. With the Great Depression at its worst and jobs impossible to find, Ahearne had no difficulty enticing the British-born players to play hockey for $50 a week in his London and District league.

In the 1936 Olympics in Garmish-Partenkirchen, Germany, the team of British-born Canadians beat Canada 2–1, largely due to the marvelous

MONTREAL MAROONS HOCKEY TEAM

WORLD'S CHAMPIONS
HOLDERS OF THE STANLEY CUP 1934-1935

T. GORMAN Man.

TOE BLAKE   CY WENTWORTH   LIONEL CONACHER   ALEX CONNELL   STEW EVANS   EARL ROBINSON   BILL MILLER
DAVE TROTTIER   JIMMIE WARD   BALDY NORTHCOTT   HOOLEY SMITH CAPT   RUSS BLINCO   ALLAN SHIELDS
SAMMY McMANUS   GUS MARKER   DUTCH GAINOR   BOB GRACIE   HERB CAIN   BILL McKENZIE

Above: To represent Britain in the 1936 Olympics, Bunny Ahearne, a British businessman, shrewdly recruited Canadian hockey players who had been born in the British Isles and brought to Canada as infants. Stunningly, the Brits won the gold medal.

Above right: The Montreal Maroons, winners of the Stanley Cup for 1934–35 season, folded after the 1937–38 campaign.

work of Jimmy Foster in the Brits' net. A pleasant blond fellow with a mustache, Foster is remembered as one of the three best goalies produced on Winnipeg rinks, the other two being Charlie Gardiner and Terry Sawchuk.

World War II's outbreak in 1939 ended Olympic hockey until the games resumed in 1948 at St. Moritz. The war also interrupted a new international event, the World Championships, which were inaugurated in 1930 by the International Ice Hockey Federation. Games were scheduled annually in the three years between Olympics.

For the second World Championships in 1931 in Krynica, Poland, Canada sent the Varsity Grads from the University of Manitoba. In goal for the Winnipeggers was Art Puttee, who that year became the only goalie in the history of international hockey not to allow a goal for an entire series. After five straight shutouts, the Grads went home with the gold.

In subsequent years Canada sent the Port Arthur Bearcats, the Toronto National Sea Fleas, the Saskatoon Quakers, the Winnipeg Monarchs, the Kimberly Dynamiters, the Sudbury Wolves, and the Trail Smoke Eaters, the latter playing in 1939 in what turned out to be the last tournament before the World War II.

Despite the prowess of their delegates, Canadians at home were not much interested in international hockey. Not until the Soviet Union emerged in 1954 as a hockey power did Canadians start to pay attention. Instead, national interest in the 1930s was focused on the NHL, which had absorbed the stars of the fallen Western leagues. Eddie Shore, known as the Edmonton Express, went to the Boston Bruins, and Bullet Joe Simpson went to the New York Americans. Even Lester Patrick himself signed on. Having ended his West Coast activities, Patrick was free to displace a fiery though virtually unknown Torontonian named Conn Smythe as coach of the New York Rangers.

Smythe had been hired in 1926 to assemble a team for Madison Square Garden to be called the Rangers. Why the Rangers? Their original name was Tex's Rangers, after Tex Rickard, the Garden president, but that name didn't survive, and neither did Smythe, who was dismissed when the more highly regarded Lester Patrick became available. Later that season, Smythe fast-talked enough backers in Toronto to raise $160,000 to buy the local NHL team, the St. Pats. He

Foster Hewitt was the voice of hockey from 1923 to 1972. With his trademark "Hello Canada," Hewitt brought hockey to fans across the continent. Perched in his gondola high atop Maple Leaf Gardens, Hewitt would start his broadcast at the beginning of the second period. He popularized the phrase "He shoots, he scores!" and is a true broadcasting legend. Hewitt was inducted into the Hall of Fame in 1965.

Clancy was an all-star defenseman for the Leafs, a fiery little fellow filled with guts, laughter, spirit, and profanity who provided inspiration for his teammates.

changed the name to the Maple Leafs to give the team a broader appeal, and began his long reign as Toronto's hockey boss and an outspoken bigwig in the league itself.

Smythe wasn't a big man but he could dominate a room. He had an intimidating voice and bright-blue eyes that could be warm and welcoming or, in an instant, cold as December. In winter he set off his outdoor wear with a distinguished off-white Borsalino hat and grey spats. In all seasons he was a force of nature, whether he was raising money or yelling at a newspaperman whose copy he disliked.

Perhaps the shrewdest move Smythe ever made, once he got the spotless and elegant Maple Leaf Gardens built in 1931, was to hire Foster Hewitt to broadcast his team's home games. Smythe had listened to Hewitt's broadcasts from the tiny Mutual Street Arena that preceded the Gardens. What impressed Smythe most happened one night in 1928, when Hewitt told listeners that if they sent 10 cents to cover handling they would receive a Maple Leaf hockey program. The response was astounding. Bag after bag of mail was piled on and around Hewitt's desk. Hewitt came to think that this evidence of radio's appeal was the major factor in Smythe's decision (a) to convince Gardens directors that broadcasts would help attendance rather than hurt it, and (b) to hire Hewitt.

Smythe loved thoroughbred racing, and his luck at the track financed significant parts of his hockey career. With the proceeds of a couple of bets in 1928, he bought the St. Pats, and with more big winners in 1930 he wrested King Clancy from the financially stressed Ottawa Senators. Clancy was one of the best and most popular players in the history of Toronto hockey, and when he died in 1986 he was still with the team, as a vice president in charge of doing anything anybody could think of for him to do.

It was fortunate, too, that Smythe operated at a time when the recruitment of players was not governed by draft rules. He was able to corral such Toronto youngsters as the flamboyant defenseman Red Horner, a tough checker, and three forwards who later formed the renowned Kid Line: Charlie Conacher, Busher Jackson, and Joe Primeau.

In the Smythe era the NHL underwent many changes. Teams in Ottawa, Philadelphia, Pittsburgh, and St. Louis dropped by the wayside. By 1942 the old ten-team lineup had been reduced to a stable, six-team league composed of Detroit, New York, Chicago, Toronto, Montreal, and Boston—a roster that would last 25 years.

In those unsettled times of depression and war, hockey was an often memorable spectacle. Art Ross, the Boston boss, once designed a game-opening ceremony featuring his dynamic defenseman Eddie Shore. For his team's entrance before the start of the game, Ross had the arena darkened. Then a band struck up "Hail to the Chief" and from the end of the rink Shore emerged under a spotlight, a toreador's cape around his shoulders. At center ice a uniformed valet lifted the cloak as the crowd screamed in delight or derision.

Then one night the Americans went into Boston with little Rabbit McVeigh in the lineup. After the theater of Shore's entrance, the Amerk players carried a large, rolled rug to mid-ice and unrolled it, disclosing McVeigh reclining like Cleopatra in Caesar's tent, his head on his palm. McVeigh then leaped to his feet, pirouetted, and blew kisses to the crowd. After that, Shore went on the ice with the rest of the Bruins.

In 1930, when the NHL began selecting all-star teams, Shore made eight of the first nine teams. He was a great, headlong, fearless, rushing defenseman who survived numerous crushing injuries that would have discouraged a less rugged man. He broke his hip one time, his collarbone another. When he cracked and displaced a spinal vertebra, he was in traction for six months. His nose was broken at least ten times, and his jaw five times, and he lost most of his teeth.

Once, his ear was mangled in a collision and the club doctor said he couldn't save it. Shore stormed from the rink, searching out a doctor's

Referee Clancy helps Detroit defenseman Jimmy Orlando find his way following a fight in which Toronto's Gaye Stewart crowned Orlando with his stick, wood-chopper style.

King Clancy was involved one way and another with the Maple Leafs from the early 1930s until his death in 1986. As a player, coach, and even as a referee he became a hockey icon.

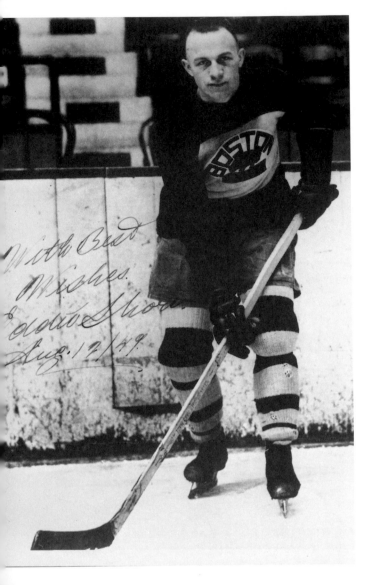

shingle. In the first two offices he visited, doctors confirmed the club doctor's opinion. The third doctor thought he could save the ear. He reached for an anaesthetic, but Shore stopped him.

"Just give me a mirror, Doc," he said. "I want to be sure you sew it on right."

Shore gave almost as much punishment as he got, which made him no favorite on the road. Still, Kyle Crichton wrote in the old *Collier's* magazine that Shore was the greatest drawing card in hockey. "What makes him that way is the hope, entertained by spectators in all cities but Boston, that he will some night be severely killed."

Shore was the culprit in a 1933 game in Boston in an incident involving Toronto's Irvin (Ace) Bailey. The story was many times retold long after both men were dead. Shore was returning to his defense position from the Toronto end, where he had lost the puck. Bailey, standing at the Toronto blue line, had his back to Shore. With a sweep of his stick Shore whacked Bailey's skates as he went by. Bailey flew into the air and came down on his back, landing head first and splitting his skull.

He nearly died. Bailey was in a Boston hospital for six weeks and his hockey career was finished. A benefit was held for him at Maple Leaf Gardens, and the highlight came when Bailey shook Shore's hand. For many years after, Bailey worked as timekeeper for NHL games in the Gardens.

Shore had been with the Bruins for 11 years in 1937 when Art Ross put together one of the game's finest forward lines, a threesome of German descent from Kitchener, Ontario—Milt Schmidt, Woody Dumart, and Bobby Bauer. Inevitably, they were called the Kraut Line, or simply the Krauts. In 1939 that line helped Shore acquire his second Stanley Cup ring, after which he had one last go-round with the fading New York Americans before he retired. With Canada in World War II, the Krauts finished one, two, three in NHL scoring in 1941. Right afterwards, the three of them enlisted in the Royal Canadian Air Force. They went overseas together and didn't return to the Bruins until the '45–'46 season. A year later the line broke up when Bauer retired.

An earlier version of the Bruins was involved in one of two marathon playoff games unlikely ever to be duplicated. In April 1933, Boston and

Toronto went on and on and on, all the way to a sixth overtime period, playing the equivalent of almost three full games. Hour after hour the game was scoreless. Shortly past midnight Conn Smythe sent word to Foster Hewitt in the broadcast booth to tell listeners that they were welcome to come down to the Gardens and see the rest of the game for free. Night owls filtered in and out as the game ground on endlessly. Finally, after 164 minutes and 46 seconds of actual playing time, right-winger Ken Doraty got a pass from lanky Andy Blair and put the puck past Tiny Thompson, the Boston goaltender.

Through it all Lorne Chabot, the Toronto goaltender, a tall lean fellow with bushy black eyebrows who wore a black baseball cap to control a heavy crown of dark hair, had turned away every Bruin puck. Years later, Bill Durnan, a goaltender of Chabot's size and shape, told friends that overtime games were especially hard on goalies: their sweat made the thick pads increasingly heavy. "A guy can easily add 40 pounds," Durnan said.

Chabot wasn't through going into the record books. Three years later, on March 24, 1936, the longest NHL game in history was played, and Lorne, wearing his baseball cap and this time a Montreal Maroons uniform, was again in the nets. By the time Modere (Mud) Bruneteau of Detroit scored the game's only goal in the sixth overtime period, Chabot had been on his skates for 176 minutes and 30 seconds of actual playing time—a feat of prodigious stamina.

That Forum game was Chabot's farewell. He saw limited action the following season as a goaltender for the New York Americans. After that season he hung up those sweat-soaked pads for good. He wasn't alone. As the Great Depression took a shattering toll on the economy, both teams that Chabot played on in the final two years of his career were forced to fold—the Americans in New York and the Maroons in hockey-mad Montreal.

Then, in 1939, a new era of upheaval confronted the game: World War II.

Above: Charlie Conacher, Joe Primeau, and Harvey (Busher) Jackson became Toronto's Kid Line by accident. They got the name by accident, too, sportswriters referring to them, because of their youth, as Toronto's "new kid" line. They got so good they acquired capital letters.

Below: Lorne Chabot was Toronto's goaltender when the Leafs won their first Stanley Cup in 1932. Beetle-browed Chabot played in the two longest games in Stanley Cup history.

Opposite top: Eddie Shore was an all-time all-timer on the Boston defense––tough, eager, fearless.

Opposite bottom: A benefit for Irvin (Ace) Bailey brought an all-star NHL lineup to Toronto to play the home side. Bailey was back from death's door where he had been dumped from behind by Boston defense star Eddie Shore. Bailey fell backward and landed on the ice on his head, splitting it open and ending his hockey career.

The war years and the period immediately before them took a large bite out of a struggling National Hockey League. The Montreal Maroons were gone after the 1937–38 season, followed after the 1941–42 season by the Brooklyn Americans, originally called the New York Americans. The Original Six was born—and has the NHL ever enjoyed a greater explosion of Hall of Fame talent than when the Montreal Canadiens, Toronto Maple Leafs, Detroit Red Wings, New York Rangers, Boston Bruins, and the Chicago Black Hawks (now Blackhawks) were meeting as often as 14 times during the regular season? The league had been reduced to its fewest number of teams since the mid-'20s, but The Original Six eventually delivered memories for the ages.

Not immediately, of course, because the war years had cut deeply into its talent pool. Historians have written that as many as 75 of the NHL's 120 players had gone into the services, many among them established stars who were impossible to replace. By the time the league had been reduced to six teams, the Rangers had lost the Colville brothers, Neil and Mac, among others. The Kraut Line (Milt Schmidt, Bobby Bauer, and Woody Dumart) was gone from Boston. Every team lost players, and, with rare exceptions, the remaining talent amounted to little more than a stream—compared to the raging river it was to become when the boys came marching home.

Legislation had to be introduced while so many of the league's best players were fighting for the survival of democracy. Travel restrictions forced the cancellation of overtime. All the while, teams continued to lose star players to the services, which meant that The Original Six during those years was caught in a waiting game for many of its biggest names to return at war's end.

For almost two decades, starting in 1942, the Stanley Cup was won by only three teams. The Canadiens won it eight times, the Maple Leafs six times and the Detroit Red Wings, five. In truth, The Original Six had become

Conn Smythe's drive and enthusiasm got Maple Leaf Gardens built in 1931 and in the following decades he ran the colorful Maple Leafs. Here he is playing host to a young Princess Elizabeth at the Gardens.

a two-tier league, with Montreal, Toronto, and Detroit blessed with the best talent. They brought the biggest stars and most passion to the arenas.

The Pony Line of Max and Doug Bentley and Bill Mosienko arrived after Chicago won the Stanley Cup in 1938. With the legendary Lester Patrick as their manager and Frank Boucher as coach, the New York Rangers were winners in 1940 with players such as the Colvilles, Lynn and Muzz Patrick, and Bryan Hextall.

Above: The Brooklyn Americans followed the Maroons when, after the 1941–42 season, they too left the NHL.

Left The Kraut Line––Milt Schmidt, Bobby Bauer and Woody Dumart––were three players of German origin from the Kitchener, Ontario, area who starred for the Boston Bruins in the 1930s and 1940s.

Above: Toronto Goalie Turk Broda stabs the puck out of mid-air with his glove hand.

Top: The Pony Line: Max and Doug Bentley and Bill Mosienko were the top scoring line of the 1946–47 season. Max Bentley led the league in scoring both seasons the line played together.

Above: Ted Kennedy of the Maple Leafs autographs a stick for a young fan.

Boston won the Cup the following year with Bill Cowley, Dit Clapper, Frank Brimsek, Bauer, Schmidt, and Dumart, but Toronto, Detroit, and Montreal were to establish a stranglehold on hockey's ultimate prize for the next 19 years. The Maple Leafs were led by a group of brilliant stars such as Turk Broda, Syl Apps, and Ted Kennedy. Detroit had Gordie Howe, Sid Abel, Terry Sawchuk, and Ted Lindsay. In Montreal, Bill Durnan was in the nets, while its best forward line comprised the Punch Line of Toe Blake, Elmer Lach, and the legendary Maurice Richard.

Top: Leafs Captain Syl Apps looks on as Turk Broda and teammates prepare for battle. A far cry from the luxurious dressing rooms of modern teams, during the Original Six era only the most basic facilities were available to players.

Above: Syl Apps was one of many NHL players who joined up during WWII. Shown here with some fellow servicemen.

Below right: Elmer Lach was the center between Toe Blake and Rocket Richard on the famous Punch Line of the 1940s.

Opposite: Bill Durnan of the Canadiens and Turk Broda of the Leafs congratulate each other after a hard-fought game. Broda won five Stanley Cups with the Leafs and Durnan two with the Canadiens. Both are now members of the HHOF.

Historians have always linked Howe and Richard. Who was the better player? Who left a greater imprint on the broad landscape of The Game during the Original Six years? Who appealed more to the fans—and why? Who was more valuable to his team?

Howe performed at a high level much longer than Richard: his 1,767 games almost doubled Richard's 978. Richard retired at age 39, Howe played until he was 52. Howe was on four Stanley Cup teams with the Red Wings, Richard on eight with the Canadiens. Howe won the scoring title (Art Ross Trophy) six times, Richard never. Howe was named the NHL's most valuable player (Hart Trophy) six times, Richard only once. Howe was on the NHL's first all-star team twelve times, Richard eight. Howe scored 801 goals and 1,049 assists, dwarfing Richard's 544 goals and 421 assists.

So who was better? Who was embraced more by the public? Clearly, Howe was the better all-around player, but Richard generated more

Top left: Ted Lindsay drives to the net against the Toronto Maple Leafs. Known as "Terrible" Ted Lindsay, he was a fierce competitor who never backed down from a fight. Hated in other arenas around the league, the Detroit star took it as a sign of respect when he was booed by opposing fans.

Bottom left: Ted Lindsay circles back for a rebound in a 1947 game against Toronto.

Above: Gordie Howe fires the puck past Toronto's Johnny Bower as defenseman Allan Stanley tries to pull him down.

Right: The Production Line. Early in his career Gordie Howe played on a line with Ted Lindsay and Sid Abel. Tough competitors, their consistent point production earned them their name.

excitement. For all of the right reasons, each has a special place in NHL history. Mention Howe, and the first word that comes to mind is durability. Richard had already stunned the hockey establishment with his 50 goals in 50 games in 1944–45 when the 18-year-old Howe joined the Red Wings in 1946, but nobody in any sport approaches the 32 years he played, 25 with the Wings. Those who played with and against him like to recall that he was all sticks and elbows, a horse of a man who owned the corners or, for that matter, any other part of the ice where he chose to establish squatter's rights. The corners belonged to him, and so did the crease, the blueline, the boards … and heaven help the man who intruded on his space. The history of The Original Six contains countless stories of the punishment he inflicted on opponents with fists, sticks, and elbows.

He was to become the most prolific goal-scorer of his time, starting in those early years on the Production Line with Abel and Lindsay. The legend that was Howe, though, almost came to an abrupt and tragic ending in the first game of the playoffs in 1950, a season in which Lindsay, Abel, and Howe finished one-two-three (Richard was No. 4) among the NHL's point-getters.

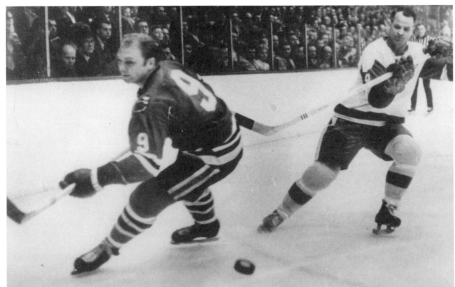

Howe was chasing Toronto's Ted Kennedy, who brought up his stick to protect himself from being hit. The blade caught Howe in the face, broke his nose and cheekbone and, far worse, sent him head-first into the Detroit Olympia boards.

A few hours later, he was on the operating table. His skull was fractured and hospital officials feared for his life. Members of his family were flown in from Saskatoon to be at his bedside, and weeks were to pass before he was allowed to leave the hospital. Wouldn't you know it: he was at the Olympia to watch his Red Wings win the Stanley Cup.

Opposite top: Howe picks the five hole on Kings goalie Wayne Rutledge.

Opposite middle: Using a straight blade, the ambidextrous Howe could shoot either right- or left-handed depending on where the defense was located.

Opposite bottom: Two of the greatest, Bobby Hull and Gordie Howe clash during this 1965 game in Chicago.

Above: Gordie Howe charges in on Montreal goaltender Gump Worsley.

Right: Gordie Howe and linemate Alex Delecchio relax in the dressing room between periods.

After over 34 years as a professional hockey player, Gordie Howe ended his NHL career after the 1979–80 season, as a member of the Hartford Whalers.

Howe wasn't the explosive performer Richard became. It wasn't how many goals Richard scored, it was the way he scored them, and even Howe has always happily acknowledged that "there was nobody like Richard for putting the puck in the net." For his part, Richard has always admitted that he wasn't in Howe's class as an all-around player. Richard skated with a choppy style, while Howe's stride was so fluid, some of his opponents perceived him to be a "lazy" skater— until, that is, they tried to catch him. Suffice to say that Howe and Richard were each one of a kind during their Original Six years.

The Rocket's best years were already behind him when I started covering the Canadiens at the start of the 1955–56 season. By then, after 13 NHL seasons, he had lost a step. He was now fighting the battle of the bulge, carrying weight he found increasingly difficult to lose. But now and then in his last five seasons, he was once again the Rocket. On those nights, there was no finer sight anywhere this game was played.

It goes beyond the stunning numbers: his 544 goals in 18 seasons, eight Stanley Cups, 82 playoff goals, and 6 overtime goals that still stand as an NHL record. All these achievements don't begin to describe the fire and fury of Richard—and what he meant to hockey in general and the Canadiens in particular. Winning at any cost was his nature. He was prepared to pay the price for every goal he scored.

Boston's "Sugar Jim" Henry congratulates Maurice
Richard. After leaving the game with a head injury, Richard
returned to score the winning goal. With blood seeping
from his bandaged head Richard raced up the boards, beat
the defenseman, and fired the puck into the Boston net.

Goals such as his 83 regular-season winners. Goals that lifted spectators out of their seats everywhere he played, because he was as much an attraction on the road as he was at the Montreal Forum. At any moment, anywhere, he could erupt with another big goal or an explosion of temper which got him into trouble with constituted authority more often than he would have liked. Through it all, good and bad, he attracted a lot of attention.

Take the night of March 23, 1944, when the Canadiens played host to the Toronto Maple Leafs in the second game of their best-of-seven Stanley Cup semi-final. The Richard who was to burst into full flower the following season, when he became the first player in NHL history to score 50 goals in 50 games, had shown what he was all about in the 1943–44 season. He had scored 23 of his 32 regular-season goals in his previous 22 games. (A dislocated shoulder sidelined Richard for four games of the Canadiens' stunning 38–5–7 season, which included a 22–0–3 home record.)

He would be getting special attention from the Toronto Maple Leafs on this March night, since the Leafs had upset the Canadiens 3–1 in Game 1 two nights earlier. The Leafs' best defensive forward, Bob Davidson,

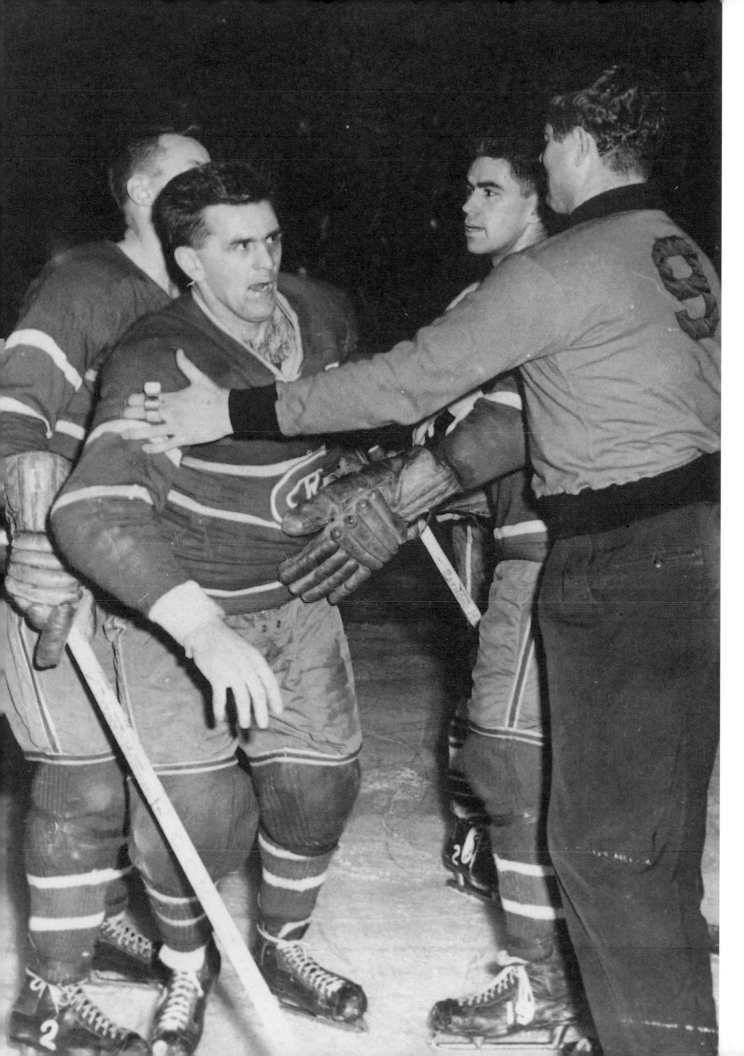

Opposite top: Shown here hugging the Stanley Cup, Rocket Richard won the trophy eight times in his 18-year career and was selected an All-Star 14 times.

Opposite bottom: Clarence Campbell stands between Jacques Plante and Rocket Richard after the Canadiens won the Cup in the 1959–60 season.

Left: Known for his explosive temper, Rocket Richard is restrained by a linesman during a 1954 game against Toronto.

49

Winning a combined 19 cups between them, Maurice and Henri Richard are one of the best brother combinations ever to play the game: the Rocket and the Pocket Rocket. Maurice was a goal scorer, Henri a gifted skater and passer. Both brothers played their entire careers in Montreal.

drew the assignment. His instructions: go everywhere Richard goes. Don't let him out of your sight.

Richard couldn't shake loose from Davidson's coverage in the first period, but Richard left the Leafs—and Davidson—reeling with three goals in the second period. He added another two in the third in what was to become the greatest individual performance in NHL playoff history: Maurice Richard 5, Toronto 1.

Until that night, only Newsy Lalonde had ever scored five goals in a playoff game. The Canadiens eliminated the Leafs with victories in the next three games and then swept the Chicago Blackhawks in four. Richard was scoring 12 goals in nine playoff games that season, the Canadiens won their first Stanley Cup in 13 seasons, and the marvelous legend of Maurice "Rocket" Richard was born.

It wasn't supposed to happen so soon. In truth, some hockey people felt it would never happen. Too brittle, they said. Injury-prone, they muttered. The problems started in 1940, when Richard was invited to the training camp of the Canadiens Seniors, a minor-league pro team. He made the team, assisted on a goal in the first regular-season game, then was sidelined for the rest of the season with a broken ankle after catching his skate in a rut in the third period.

The following year, he played well for the first 30 games, suffered a broken wrist

Above: Eyes wide, Rocket Richard is the first player to react to a loose puck in front of Toronto netminder Johnny Bower.

Following pages:
The Rocket's intensity shone through his eyes.

"Big Jean" battles with a defenseman in front of the Bruins net. One of the first players to combine size and strength with a fluid stride and a goal scorer's touch, Beliveau remains one of the greatest athletes in hockey history.

in his 31st, missed the rest of the regular season, but returned to score six goals in four playoff games.

The 1942–43 season was his first with the Canadiens: this time he fractured his right ankle.

Three major injuries in three years: maybe, just maybe, he was indeed too brittle to play in the NHL.

The 1943–44 season erased those fears, but even that Stanley Cup year was eclipsed by his stunning, and the NHL's first-ever, 50-goals-in-50-games season in 1945—albeit in a league that was still waiting for many of its star players to return from the war. Three days after Christmas, Richard scored five goals and assisted on three others in a 9–1 victory over the Detroit Red Wings. Remarkably, he scored 43 goals in his first 38 games and, in Toronto the following week, tied Joe Malone's record of 44 goals, which was achieved in a 22-game season.

A week later, the same teams were at the Forum, and nobody needed a road map to understand that the Maple Leafs, as a group, were prepared to do anything to prevent Richard from scoring his 45th. With nine games remaining in the season, Richard, assuming he stayed healthy, was certain to eclipse Malone's record. The Leafs didn't regard that as a problem—as long as Richard's 45th goal of the season wasn't scored against the Leafs.

It's why Richard had Davidson on him. Nick Metz also stayed close to him, but with roughly four minutes remaining in the game, linemate Toe Blake caught Richard with a pass and, in one motion, he one-timed it at Frank McCool. Goal!

Eight games remained in the season, so now the question was: could he reach the magic 50? If so, when? If not, why not?

Above: Toe Blake celebrates with Jean Beliveau, Bobby Rousseau, and the rest of the Montreal Canadiens after winning the Stanley Cup.

Left: One of the smoothest players ever to play the game, Jean Beliveau was a gentleman on and off the ice. Beliveau retired with over 500 goals and 1000 points. He won ten Stanley Cups as a Canadiens player and seven more as a member of their front office.

Above: Beliveau scores his 500th goal against the Minnesota North Stars on February 11, 1971.

Right: Rocket Richard shares a laugh with Bernie "Boom Boom" Geoffrion after he scored his 50th goal. Geoffrion is credited with being the inventor of the slapshot.

Not surprisingly, Richard did it the hard way. He was sitting on 49 goals when the Canadiens played their final home game of the season. Late in the game, he was awarded a penalty shot—and missed!

The Canadiens traveled to Boston for the season's final regular-season game. The Bruins were leading 2–1 with fewer than three minutes remaining. Dutch Hiller had scored the only Montreal goal 8.24 into the second period, but now all the attention was on Richard. Time was running out, and so was his pursuit of his 50th. Elmer Lach collided with Boston goaltender Harvey Bennett, leaving Richard with what amounted to an empty net for the milestone goal.

Even with Richard holding their banner aloft, the Canadiens were not the dominant team in the decade after the end of World War II. Although they won the Stanley Cup in 1946, it wasn't until 1953 that the Canadiens were to win their next one, finally ushering in a decade that did belong to them.

The 1955–56 season was to see the birth of the NHL's greatest dynasty, which didn't end until the Canadiens had won five consecutive Stanley Cups—a record likely to stand for all time. They were this dominant: 12 of the players were to play on all five teams. Jacques Plante was the goaltender, Doug Harvey was the leader on defense. The forwards included Maurice and Henri Richard, Jean Beliveau, Bernard Geoffrion and Dickie Moore—all eventually inducted into the Hockey Hall of Fame.

Over the years, hockey people have debated which of the game's dynasties was the greatest. Was it the Canadiens of the last half of the '50s? The Canadiens team that won four consecutive Stanley Cups in the late '70s? How about the New York Islanders of the early '80s? They won four in a row and made it to the Stanley Cup final for a fifth consecutive year before falling to the Edmonton Oilers, who started another dynasty with the matchless talents of Wayne Gretzky, Mark Messier, Paul Coffey, Grant Fuhr, Jari Kurri, Glenn Anderson, and others.

The reality is that it's impossible to compare dynasties from different eras. The Original Six Canadiens had to win only two playoffs series; post-expansion teams had to win more. On the other hand, no team

Henri Richard flies along the boards of the Montreal Forum.

Protesters picketed outside the Forum awaiting League President Clarence Campbell's arrival at Montreal's third last regular season game of 1955.

dominated the playoffs as much as the Canadiens, who were to win nine Stanley Cups between 1946 and 1966.

None was more dominant than the team that won its fifth in a row in 1959–60. The Canadiens swept Chicago in the semi-final, outscoring the Blackhawks 14–6. They outscored the Maple Leafs, 15–5 in four games. Plante had shutouts in three of the eight games. That particular Cup triumph was also to be Richard's last. He was in training camp that fall, but after one morning practice during which he scored four goals in a scrimmage, he retired from the game. Hockey had lost its brightest star and most controversial superstar. The people had lost an icon.

He was, after all, much more than just a hockey player. He could lift a team, a province and, at times, even a country into a frenzy of winning. He pushed himself to the brink. When he and the Canadiens won, people felt they too had won; when the Canadiens lost, they lost. It's why Montrealers erupted into what will always be remembered as the Richard Riot on March 17, 1955, after Richard was suspended by NHL president Clarence Campbell for the last few games of the regular season and for the playoffs after a stick-swinging altercation with Boston Bruins player Hal Laycoe.

If Richard was the soul of these great Canadiens teams, even long after he was able to score goals the way he once did, then coach Toe Blake was their conscience and father figure.

Players will tell you that they don't see their coaches lacing up their skates at game time. It's up to the players to get the job done and nobody else. Blake was an exception.

His players didn't merely respect him during his 13 seasons behind the Canadiens bench, which produced eight Stanley Cups: they feared him. It's true that he coached at a time when, for the most part, there was no National Hockey League Players Association. There had been a surprise and, as it developed, failed effort to form a union in the late '50s, with players such as Detroit's Lindsay and the Canadiens' Harvey taking a leading role, but in a matter of only days, the Red Wings withdrew, leaving behind nothing more than a Players' Council. The group met occasionally with the owners but accomplished little until

Above: Maurice Richard holds a press conference to appeal for calm after the rioting in Montreal that resulted from his 1955 playoff suspension for hitting an official.

Left: The streets outside the Montreal Forum were littered with debris after the 1955 Richard Riot. The rampaging fans caused $500,000 in property damage.

Toe Blake celebrates another Cup victory flanked by David Molson (left) and Sam Pollock (right).

June 1967, when Toronto lawyer Alan Eagleson organized the players.

Blake was blessed with hockey's best players, but what made him special was his talent for getting the best out of the best—much as his pupil, Scotty Bowman, got from another Canadiens dynasty in the late '70s. Among coaches, Blake was always a step ahead of his peers in most games and, not incidentally, several steps ahead of his players. Frank Mahovlich, an 18-season veteran of the NHL, was one of Blake's greatest admirers, even though he never played for him. He felt Blake was responsible for 50 percent of what was needed to win.

"I've always felt that a good coach is the one who wins," Blake agreed. "But 50 percent? If that had been the case with me, my teams would have won a lot more games … more Cups."

"There are 20 guys in a dressing room," goaltender Gump Worsley once said, "and it's seldom you find even two of them alike. Toe knew each individual—the ones who worked from the needles, the ones who needed another approach. Between periods, he never blasted an individual. He'd say some guys aren't pulling their weight. The guys who weren't doing the job knew who he was talking about and you'd see the heads droop. But he'd never embarrass anyone in front of everyone. His ability to handle players—I guess that's what made him great."

That's not to say that the great coach didn't have his likes and dislikes. Jacques Plante, who Blake always insisted was the best goaltender he'd ever seen during the five consecutive years the Canadiens won the Stanley Cup, was not among his favorites. In time, Blake was chiefly responsible for getting Plante moved to the New York Rangers in 1963—but not before Plante was responsible for introducing a piece of equipment that revolutionized hockey.

The Canadiens were in New York to face the Rangers on Nov. 1, 1959. A little more than three minutes into the first period, Rangers right-winger

Toronto coach Punch Imlach encourages his troops from behind the Maple Leafs bench.

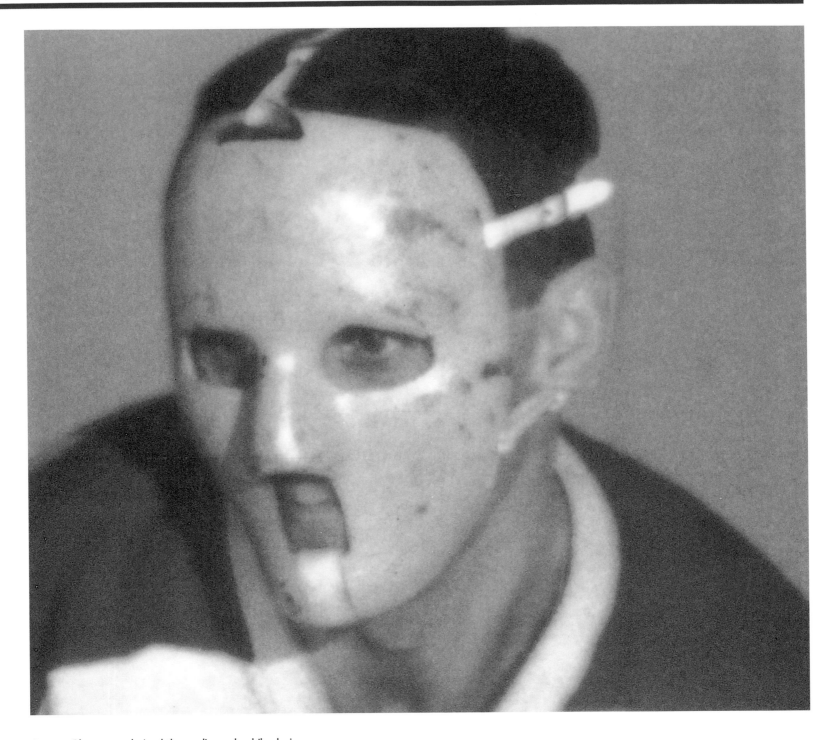

Jacques Plante popularized the goalie mask while playing
for the Canadians in the 1950s and 60s.

Andy Bathgate moved in on a crouching Plante. He lifted a short back-hander into the goaltender's face, opening a savage cut that ran in a crooked line from the corner of his mouth, along his cheek, and through his nostril.

Moments later, Plante was helped from the ice and, eventually, to the medical room. Twenty minutes later, Plante made his way to the Canadiens dressing room, where Blake awaited him.

"How bad is it?" Blake asked.

"It's sore," was the reply.

"Why don't you wear your mask for the rest of the game," suggested Blake.

"I don't think I can go back in without it," said Plante.

The sight of Plante skating onto the ice wearing a mask drew a buzz of wonderment from the Madison Square Garden audience. In truth, though, it wasn't a surprise to those among us who covered the team. He had been making small noises about wearing the mask in a game for several weeks. He argued: was it really necessary for goaltenders to stand there while pucks came at them from every direction? Players were shooting harder. They were working curves into the blades of their sticks. Why not a face-fitting mask? Blake resisted the idea: his argument was that goaltenders would find it difficult to track a puck lying at their feet.

"He can practice with one if he wants," Blake had said, "but no goal-tender of mine is gonna wear one in a game. We're here to win."

Plante stopped 28 of the 29 shots he faced in that game wearing the mask. Blake didn't like it, but the mask was born.

Among the great stars of the Original Six were Bobby Hull and Stan Mikita.

Hull was, in every way, a franchise player. His fearsome shot, strength, and uncommon good looks brought the fans back to Chicago Stadium in sellout numbers after too many seasons of empty seats and losing teams. Before his arrival in 1957–58 directly out of junior hockey with the St. Catharines Teepees, the Blackhawks had made the playoffs just once in 11 seasons. Hull scored only 13 goals in his rookie season,

another year in which the Blackhawks missed the playoffs. He had 18 in the second season of his 15-year career in Chicago, which included five seasons of 50 goals or more. In his fourth season, 1960–61, the Blackhawks won their first Stanley Cup since 1938, and haven't won one since. He was the Golden Jet, and fans everywhere worshipped him.

Mikita arrived a year later, also from the Teepees, and was to enjoy a Hall of Fame, 21-season career with the Blackhawks. He was a finesse center-man, who scored 541 goals and 926 assists in 1,394 games. He led the NHL in scoring four times and was named its most valuable player twice.

In the final year of The Original Six, an 18-year-old Bobby Orr lit up Boston Garden when he joined the Bruins for the 1966–67 season. Orr was part of a group of many new stars in several sports to come along in the mid-60s, the golden boys of that era. He put a new face on the way defensemen should play, and may have been the best ever to play this game. He left his mark on hockey as no player had before him. Before Orr, many of hockey's great stars skated at top speed. Others passed the puck at top speed. Many shot it at top speed. What made Orr special was that he did all of these things at top speed.

"When Orr was playing, he was somewhere up there, the rest of us were down here," Canadiens defenseman Serge Savard once remarked.

Emile Francis, who was a coach and general manager with several NHL teams recalled:

I saw a lot of Orr in junior hockey. The kids would give him the puck

Above: Hull played 15 seasons with the Blackhawks.

Left: Chicago Blackhawk stars Tony Esposito and Bobby Hull share a laugh before taking the ice.

Above: Breaking in on the Toronto goaltender, Stan Mikita tries to slip a backhand past Terry Sawchuk. Mikita entered the NHL a scrappy player willing to fight anyone who challenged him. He mellowed over the course of his career and in 1967 he became the first player to win the Art Ross Trophy, the Hart Trophy, and the Lady Byng Trophy in the same year.

Following pages:
Bobby Hull used his tremendous speed and booming shot to become a prolific goal scorer in the NHL. Routinely scoring over 50 goals a season, the "Golden Jet" rejuvenated a struggling franchise when he arrived in Chicago. The Hawks had missed the playoffs in 10 of 11 seasons before Hull's rookie season of 1957–58. By 1961 they were Stanley Cup Champions.

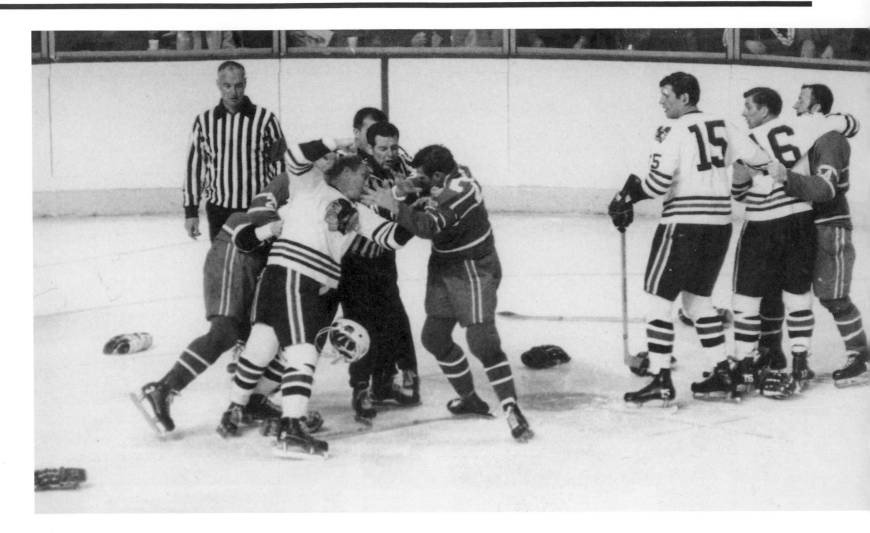

and then they'd stand around and watch. In the pros, I figured they'd throw the puck to him and then set themselves up for a return pass.

I'd look at my scoring sheet after each game against Boston, and there's Orr with six ... seven ... eight shots. One game, he had twelve. He's a defenseman," said Francis, "he's not supposed to get that many shots. But then I'd try to think how many times we'd caught him for a goal and I couldn't find it happening. I would see veterans panic in a tough spot and most of the time you couldn't blame them. Orr? He'd stand there as if he owned the place. He was some meal ticket.

Above: Bobby Hull was wearing a helmet and mask, to protect a broken jaw, when John Ferguson of the Montreal Canadiens punched him in the face. Hull's reaction was swift as he swung back at Ferguson before the helmet hit the ice.

Left: Hall of Famers Stan Mikita and Bobby Hull played together as Blackhawks from the 1958–59 season, when Mikita arrived in Chicago, until the end of the 1971–72 season when Hull joined the Winnipeg Jets of the WHA.

Boston scouts discovered Orr when he was still a 12-year old playing Bantam hockey in Parry Sound. At 14 he signed with Boston's Junior team, the Oshawa Generals, and played four years for the team before joining the Bruins at the age of 18.

Right: Johnny Bower started his professional career in the AHL in 1945–46, and played a season with the New York Rangers in 1953–54, but he didn't manage to find a permanent home in the NHL until 1958 when he was drafted by the Toronto Maple Leafs. He went on to win four Stanley Cups in Toronto.

Below: Johnny Bower clears the puck out of the Rangers' zone.

Displaying his lightning reflexes,
Sawchuk lashes out with his left leg
to kick away a shot.

Expansion was only a year down the road when Orr started weaving his special magic with the Bruins in 1966, but the reality is that the Montreal-Toronto rivals owned the '60s, winning nine Stanley Cups in the decade. They had the best players—players with fire in their eyes and hot coals in their hearts—and they had the best coaches. There was surely nothing approaching the rivalry between Canadiens coach Blake and Toronto's Punch Imlach. When you talk about the magic of this one-time Canadiens-Leafs rivalry, you're talking about Imlach and Blake. They fueled it and their players fed off it.

The Canadiens and Leafs were a day away from the start of their best-of-seven Stanley Cup final in 1967. Chicago had finished in first place with 94 points during the regular season. The Canadiens were well behind with 77, two more than the Leafs. Toronto wasn't supposed to have a chance against the Blackhawks, but the Leafs, riding the brilliant netminding wave of veterans Johnny Bower and Terry Sawchuk,

had stunned Chicago in a six-game semi-final series. The Canadiens had erased the Rangers in four.

The next night, Rogatien Vachon (who had just been called up by the Canadiens that season) was brilliant in a 6–2 victory over the Maple Leafs. He was in the nets for Games 2 and 3, both won by the Maple Leafs. Game 4 was won by the Canadiens, but the young and inexperienced Vachon was out of the series, as Imlach had promised, after two periods in Game 5. Gump Worsley didn't allow a goal in the third period after the Leafs had taken a 4–1 lead, and was the starting goaltender in Game 6. The Leafs won the Stanley Cup, handling the Canadiens 3–1.

The Original Six was also about Toronto defenseman Bobby Baun.

You won't find Baun's name among former Toronto superstars in the Hockey Hall of Fame, but perhaps a special place should have been set aside for him because of the goal he scored on an April night in 1964.

The Leafs had made it to the Stanley Cup final with a seven-game victory over the Canadiens, the eighth time the teams had met in the playoffs. Now they were facing the Detroit Red Wings, victors over Chicago in seven, but things hadn't been going as well as the Leafs had hoped. They split the first two games in Toronto. They also split the next two at Detroit, but the Red Wings stunned the Maple Leafs at the Gardens in Game 5, winning 2–1.

Game 6 was in Detroit, so everything pointed to the Red Wings putting away the Leafs for good. Things didn't get better for the Leafs when Baun stopped a slapshot with his ankle fairly late in the game, but despite urging from doctors that he call it a night, Baun—now with his ankle frozen—insisted on returning to the ice. The game went into overtime and, fewer than three minutes into it, Baun beat Terry Sawchuk with a weak long shot.

"I kinda felt sorry for (Detroit defenseman) Bill Gadsby," recalled Baun. "The puck hit him and deflected past Sawchuk."

Baun was on crutches for the next two days, then didn't miss a shift in Game 7 at the Gardens. The Leafs won, 4–0.

The next day, doctors revealed that Baun's ankle had indeed been broken. He spent the next two months on crutches.

Opposite top: At the time of his death Terry Sawchuk had recorded more victories than any other goaltender in NHL history. He won four Stanley Cups in Toronto and Detroit over the course of his brilliant career.

Opposite bottom: As a young man Sawchuk showed his talents early as a member of the Omaha Knights.

Bobby Baun circles behind the Toronto net. Baun is best remembered for scoring the winning goal, in game six of the 1964 Stanley Cup Finals, while playing on a broken ankle.

The Original Six was about Frank Mahovlich, a giant talent with the Leafs before he moved to Detroit and the Canadiens.

Things were going badly for the Maple Leafs at the Gardens. They were trailing by several goals late in the second period when Henri Richard, head down, glided toward Mahovlich, who had more than enough room to clear the puck to either side. Instead, he lifted it into Richard's face, sending the Canadiens centerman to the ice, blood spurting from an ugly cut. Dickie Moore was the first man off the Canadiens bench, quickly followed by the rest of the players, and for the next few minutes fights erupted everywhere. At period's end, Canadiens general manager Frank Selke, Sr., hurried down to the Canadiens room.

"I don't want you to put Moore on the ice for the start of the third period," he told coach Blake.

"Why not?"

"You saw what happened out there," Selke said. "I don't want any more trouble. If you send him out, we could have a riot on our hands."

"You saw what that SOB Mahovlich did," fumed Blake.

"I don't care. I don't want any more trouble. Keep Moore on the bench," Selke insisted.

"OK, but I don't like it," insisted Blake.

Above: Frank Mahovlich blows past Bruins captain Fernie Flamman on his way to the Boston net.

Left: Glenn Hall played in 502 consecutive NHL games, earning the name "Mr. Goalie."

Opposite: The Big M, Frank Mahovlich, has his feet cut out from under him as Detroit goalie Terry Sawchuk kicks his pad at the puck.

Above: Dave Keon, the longtime Leafs captain, was one of the best two-way players to ever play the game. He spent 15 seasons in Toronto and won four Stanley Cups with the Leafs.

"Do it," snapped Selke.

Moore was on the ice for the start of the third period.

The Original Six was about Dave Keon. Keon was to be the Leafs' captain for six years and, arguably, the team's most valuable player during the 15 seasons he played in Toronto. He killed the opposition with his speed and was as dangerous on defense as he was offensively. He was one of the NHL's many small players during that era, but nobody was blessed with a larger heart. You'd find him in the corners and in heavy traffic in front of the nets. You'd find him everywhere, flitting here and there with the grace of a butterfly.

How do you forget the overtime goal scored by Toronto's Bill Barilko, which won the Stanley Cup in 1951? Or that the Leafs won the Stanley Cup that year in five games, each one in overtime?

The Original Six surely was about Conn Smythe, the Leafs owner who built the Gardens, as well as his son Stafford, and his partner, Harold Ballard. Conn, the father, was a dynamo. He was feared by everyone, including his players. No one was spared the acid in his tongue: not friends, not family, not any of the owners of the other five teams.

The Original Six was about Sam Pollock, who came out of the Canadiens' minor league system, replaced Selke as the team's general manager in 1964, then led the franchise to nine Stanley Cups in 14 seasons. He was so highly regarded, the NHL's leaders often approached him for advice in matters which affected his team as well as others. "What Sam always had going for him is that he knew what was needed to win," NHL president Clarence Campbell once said.

He was as shrewd as anyone in the judgment of players, and I don't know of anyone who was more knowledgeable as to the working of the bylaws. There was an element of suspicion in Sam all the time, but in spite of the enormous input he had in the creation of what were deemed to be improvements, I'm not aware of a single situation where he designed it for his own benefit. He was very resourceful in the ways he went about some of the things, but none was off-colour, nor could you say they were the product of a scheme.

Pollock was successful before the NHL expanded from six to twelve

Previous pages, Above and Right:
Toronto Maple Leaf Bill Barilko became part of hockey folklore in 1951 after scoring the Stanley Cup winning goal against the Montreal Canadiens. Shortly after the season ended, Barilko died in a plane crash while flying to Northern Ontario for a fishing trip. It was 11 years before his body was discovered and 11 years before the Leafs would again win the Cup in 1962.

teams. He was even more successful beyond it. He has nine Stanley Cup rings because the teams he put together mirrored their general manager's approach to the game. He won more often than anyone else because he and they worked harder than anyone else.

The Original Six was about Clarence Campbell, who took over as NHL president in 1946 and held the post until 1977. Campbell was a lawyer and a Rhodes scholar who had also been a prosecutor at the Nuremberg trials. Hockey was Campbell's life and he lived it every waking moment. In many ways, it was his reason for living. He would defend it against any danger, real or imagined. Nothing else mattered. And like most people who put the game above everything else, he was unforgiving with people who, in his perception, were a threat to it. Now, Commissioner Gary Bettman rules the league and its owners. He leads, they follow. Then, Campbell was the first to admit he was merely an employee. He worked for the six owners. He followed their instructions, with no questions asked. It was the owners who pressed for expansion over Campbell's objections, but once the 12-team NHL was put in place, nobody worked harder to make that stunning growth as successful as it would become.

NHL President Clarence Campbell draws a name out of the Stanley Cup during the 1967 expansion draft.

When the 1967 Stanley Cup was awarded, the National Hockey League was nothing more than a regional group of six teams. Games were played from Montreal to New York and from Boston to Chicago. California, the Sun Belt, Western Canada, and the rest of America remained to be conquered.

The Toronto Maple Leafs were the last team of the Original Six to win a Stanley Cup. 1967 was a great year for Canada. It was the centennial of Confederation and the city of Montreal was hosting the planet with Expo 67.

With the arrival of fall, when Man and His World shut its doors, the National Hockey League opened its to the West.

Hockey would never again be the same. All at once, for the ridiculous amount by today's standards of $2 million each, six new teams were welcomed into the league. Now, hockey's fantasy world faced the challenge of trying to put the St. Louis Blues on the same pedestal as the Boston Bruins.

Children who had spent the winters buying hockey cards, knowing that they needed 125 to complete their collection, were discovering the progress of professional sports. In the future, they would need to seek the cards of players like Les Binkley and André Lacroix.

These children couldn't guess that in less than seven years, they would become exuberant fans of new heroes like Bobby Clarke, Dave Schultz, Bernie Parent and Reggie Leach, or that the Philadelphia Flyers would become the first team from the major expansion to win the Stanley cup.

While perusing the new rosters, the ordinary fan who "knew his hockey" was intrigued by the architecture of the new buildings and the colors of the new uniforms: the orange and the black of the Philadelphia Flyers, the blue and gold of the St. Louis Blues, and the yellow and green of the Oakland Seals.

Two-time Stanley Cup winner and three-time Hart
Trophy winner Bobby Clarke came to epitomize the
Philadelphia Flyers of the 1970s. Combining equal parts
skill, determination, and intimidation, Clarke and the Flyers
would beat their opponents both physically and on the
scoreboard. A gifted offensive player, Clarke broke the
100-point barrier several times early in his career. Becoming
a more complete player as his career wound on, Clarke
developed into an excellent defensive player and won the
Selke trophy in 1983.

The owners of the established clubs didn't show much generosity toward their new partners. Viewed from Montreal, the first Canadiens game against an expansion team didn't seem very exciting. Everyone expected a slaughter. How could these former American League players and those rejects from the Original Six hold up against Jean Beliveau, Bobby Hull, or Phil Esposito?

I listened to the radio broadcast of the Canadiens against the Pittsburgh Penguins, trying to envision their powder-blue uniforms. A difficult 2–1 victory: that night we realized that the minors had been full of players dreaming of an opportunity to play against the great established stars. And young coaches, such as Scotty Bowman with the St. Louis Blues, had long been waiting for a chance to use new systems that would allow less talented players to save face against those more gifted.

The finals of this first season pitted the Montreal Canadiens against the St. Louis Blues. The Canadiens won all four games but every one was a battle, every one a one-goal game. Scotty Bowman had instilled confidence in proud, gritty veterans who used the last sparks of their fire against a much more powerful team.

When it was all over, coach Toe Blake, his trademark hat screwed onto his head, announced his retirement. He had achieved his last victory against Scotty Bowman. Thirty years later, Scotty was still behind the bench breaking his mentor's records.

Bowman's admiration of Blake was sincere, so much so that several years later when he became the feared coach of the Canadiens, Scotty often invited Blake to talk to his players: "I don't want him to tell them what to do," he explained to reporters, "but they all know who Toe Blake is. They know he is a famous coach and if he praises them, if he passes along some advice, they will often listen to him more than they would to anyone else."

The sixties ended with another Stanley Cup victory for Montreal, this one going to a young coach by the name of Claude Ruel. But even though the Canadiens had won the final against Bowman's Blues for the second year in succession, their fans knew that the real menace to their dominance was to be found not in the St. Louis Arena but in Boston Garden.

The Boston Bruins had a host of fabulously talented players, but by far the best was Bobby Orr, probably the greatest defenseman of all time.

Throughout its history, hockey had seen many defensemen capable of leading the offence. We can go back to Eddie Shore, Kenny Reardon, Red Kelly, or Doug Harvey. But no defenseman had the genius or the

Doug Harvey skates for a loose puck in front of the net as Jacques Plante tries to push a Toronto forward out of his crease. Plante is credited with making the goalie mask an accepted piece of equipment. Plante had worn the mask in practice for some time, but after being cut by a shot in a 1959 game he began to wear the mask full-time and went on to win the Vezina Trophy five years in a row.

ability of Bobby Orr. Orr revolutionized hockey. He completely changed the coaches' strategy, and his electrifying style paved the way for modern defensemen.

Bruins fans stood on their seats when Orr took charge deep in his own end. He usually grabbed the puck by going around the net to his left. Then, his luxuriant hair barely dishevelled by the wind, he would lead the rush to opposition territory, outmaneuvering the left winger at the blue line.

At that moment, Phil Esposito would make his dash to join Orr, knowing that Orr would take the puck deep into the opponent's end. While Orr was blazing past the defenseman who was trying to take him into the boards, Esposito would go to the net and position himself right in front of the goaltender. In a flash, Orr could choose: try to rush to the net or pass to Esposito waiting to shoot from point-blank range.

It was a deadly combination, so much so that Orr and Esposito finished first and second in the league scoring race two years in succession. Orr took the title in 1969–70 and Esposito followed suit the next year. In the '70s, arenas weren't as large as they are today. Boston Garden was old and virtually obsolete, but also incredibly intimate. Players didn't wear helmets and the fans could recognize their favorites without having to see their numbers.

Orr could have been bald, wearing a numberless, nameless jersey,

Above: Bobby Orr circles behind the net while holding off a Montreal forechecker. Throughout his career Orr electrified crowds around the NHL with his fearless end-to-end rushes.

Below: Yvan Cournoyer follows Orr as he prepares for one of his legendary rushes.

even a white one without a crest, and any hockey aficionado would have recognized him as soon as he wound up behind his net. He was magic.

But general manager Milt Schmidt surrounded him with an array of flamboyant personalities who gave birth to the Big Bad Bruins of the '70s. Any fan not born after 1965 remembers Phil Esposito, Wayne Cashman, Carol Vadnais, Johnny Bucyk a.k.a. "The Chief," and Ken Hodge. And let's not forget goalie Gerry Cheevers, whose impressive face mask was covered with painted sutures to show where he would have been cut.

Nearly 30 years later, Carol Vadnais still fondly remembers these great players with whom he won the Stanley Cup.

Today, Vadnais does volunteer work with an association fighting against lupus, a terrible disease which afflicted his wife Raymonde. When the opportunity arises, Bobby

One of the best goal scorers in NHL history, Phil Esposito teamed with Bobby Orr in the early 1970s to form a deadly offensive duo.

Top left: Gerry Cheevers won two Stanley Cups with the Boston Bruins in 1970 and '72. He played the majority of his career with the Bruins and coached them for several seasons in the early '80s after knee injuries forced him to retire in 1980.

Bottom left: Helpless, Gerry Cheevers watches as the puck flies past him into an open net.

Above: Cheevers' mask

Bobby Orr flies through the air after
scoring on St. Louis goalie Glenn Hall
to win the Stanley Cup Finals. The
Bruins swept the expansion Blues in
four straight and Orr won the Art Ross
trophy as the NHL's regular-season
scoring leader.

Opposite: A classic Dryden pose. A very studious athlete, after his retirement Dryden went on to pen *The Game,* a best-selling book chronicling his experiences in hockey.

Orr helps his old teammate: "I've never known a leader like Bobby Orr," said Vadnais.

> He was generosity incarnate. He has always given all he could without ever asking for anything in return. When we used to travel, the door to his room was always open for a teammate who wished to talk with him. He always had beer cooling and Bobby would smile at whoever came knocking at the door. He had such tremendous talent that none of us could compare ourselves to him. Nevertheless, he was the easiest and most unaffected guy on the team.

All this from a man who was himself a participant in six All-Star games.

To this day, a large poster of Orr flying through the air in front of the St. Louis Blues goalie Glen Hall hangs in the Fleet Center in Boston. Orr had just given the Bruins their first Stanley Cup of the '70s and even before landing on the ice, he was celebrating.

The '70s Bruins came close to being a dynasty. But the Forum's ghosts and a rookie named Ken Dryden prevented them from winning three consecutive Stanley Cups.

In 1971, "Les Glorieux" ended the regular season 24 points behind the Bruins, but they called up a rookie goaltender who played in six games before the beginning of the playoffs: a Cornell graduate, future lawyer, future writer, and future general manager and president of the Toronto Maple Leafs.

The Bruins were heavily favored to defeat the Canadiens. But Ken Dryden, almost single-handedly, beat them with stops that have since become legendary.

Nineteen seventy-two—a pivotal year in hockey history. In September, the Soviet Union national team faced Team Canada. At the same time, on new ice surfaces in Quebec, Philadelphia, Winnipeg, and nine other cities, businessmen were trying to start a new major league. The World Hockey Association would turn the hockey world upside down until the end of the decade. But before that came the clash of the titans—and a shock.

Although he never played an NHL game, Vladislav Tretiak is a goaltending legend. Tretiak won three Olympic Gold Medals and ten World Championships for team USSR. His fame grew in North America during his outstanding performance in the 1972 Summit Series. Although the Soviets would lose the series on Paul Henderson's famous goal, Tretiak's legend was firmly established in the minds of all those who saw him play.

Any young Canadian knew that in 1972 the best NHL players were too strong for the amateur Soviets. This was prior to Glasnost and Perestroika. The Soviets were a mystery to the Canadians—thought of as the big bad guys, part of the KGB, professionals in disguise. But we were mostly convinced that the pros, our heroes, would inflict a terrible blow on them.

Scouts and reporters were no help to the Canadian coaches and players. They would talk about victories of 8–0 or 9–0. They said that the 20-year-old goalie, Vladislav Tretiak, was no match for Phil Esposito or Yvan Cournoyer.

On Sept. 2 1972, the Montreal Forum had an air of celebration and expectation when Prime Minister Pierre Elliott Trudeau moved forward to drop the puck for the ceremonial face-off. Finally, here was the chance to avenge every defeat at the world championships or the Olympics since the Second World War.

An occasional pessimist worried about the absence of three great Canadian stars. Bobby Orr was injured. Jean-Claude Tremblay, who had gone from the Canadiens to the Quebec Nordiques, and Bobby Hull, deserter to the Winnipeg Jets, were banished from their country's national team. Organizer Alan Eagleson was exhibiting unwavering loyalty to the NHL.

Goals from Phil Esposito and Paul Henderson in the opening minutes of the first game seemed to confirm the highest hopes. But the elation wasn't to last.

Wave after wave, the red sea was turning the game around … as well as the series. Valeri Kharlamov, Vladimir Petrov, and Alexander Yakushev, hockey virtuosos playing with the cohesion of a symphonic orchestra, threw the country into a state of shock.

The tournament was to become the series of the century and hockey would never be the same again.

In the end, Canada won the series with a record of four wins, three losses and a tie. Everyone remembers Paul Henderson's winning goal. When Canadians are asked to name a great moment in the 20th century, Henderson's goal will always be one of the things they recall. Nobody has forgotten the outburst of joy that gripped the country when viewers saw Tretiak lying on the ice and Henderson in an ecstatic embrace in the arms of Yvan Cournoyer.

The Soviets and Canada would cross paths throughout the decade.

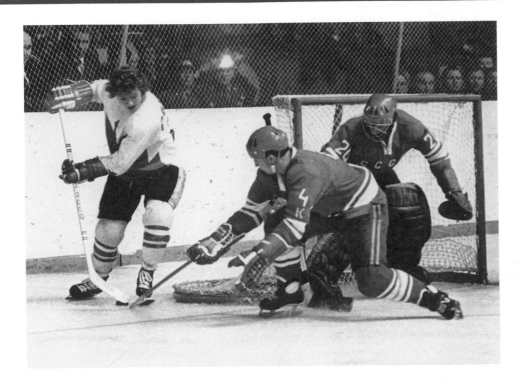

Top left: Bobby Clarke is poke-checked by a Soviet defender as he tries to work his way out from behind the net. For many fans, Clarke's toothless grin as he celebrates Canada's victory has come to symbolize the Canadian hockey player.

Bottom left: Soviet star Vladimir Kharlamov shone in international competitions between 1969 and 1980. During the 1972 Summit Series he was the subject of a great deal of controversy. He was single-handedly beating the Canadians when in Game Six Team Canada's Bobby Clarke slashed him on the ankle, knocking him out of the series. Clarke would later admit that the slash was a deliberate attempt to injure the Soviet star.

Opposite top right: Former Boston Bruins Coach Harry Sinden patrolled the bench for Canada at the 1972 Series. Retired from coaching, Sinden is now the general manager of the Boston Bruins.

Opposite bottom right: After his retirement as a player, Vladislav Tretiak joined the Chicago Blackhawks organization as a goaltending coach.

Above: Team Canada goaltender Tony Esposito dives across the net.

Left: Tretiak makes a glove save on a high shot.

Following pages: Henderson moves in on Tretiak.

Opposite: Henderson raises his arms in celebration as Tretiak tries in vain to grab the puck.

Top left: Soviet players look on stunned as Paul Henderson celebrates the most famous goal in the history of hockey. The winning goal of the 1972 Summit Series, it has become known simply as "Paul Henderson's winning goal." Played at the peak of Cold War tensions, it was the most intense and animosity-filled international series ever played.

Middle left: Henderson leaps into the arms of teammate Yvan Cournoyer immediately after scoring the winning goal in the 1972 Summit Series.

Bottom left: Ken Dryden and Team Canada celebrate after Henderson's winning goal. Playing under unbelievable pressure, Dryden would later describe the relief he felt that the series was over.

The 1974 series between the WHA and the U.S.S.R., the first Canada Cup in 1976, the Challenge Cup played in New York in 1979: all great games, great series, great tournaments that left their mark on hockey.

But the changes in the world of hockey were even deeper. While players were furiously facing off on the ice, coaches were attending conferences and seminars all over Europe. They were learning from the people who had initially come to learn. The game was being transformed, becoming an exciting mixture of the instinct-driven North-American and the collective European play. Changes were overtaking the sport. The great confrontations between the Soviets and the North-American teams, the passions they raised—this enormous shake-up of ideas and prejudices would expand the mentality of Canadians. And while the Americans viewed the people of the U.S.S.R. as mean and dangerous Communists, north of the border, the same Soviets had names and faces. Often, as in the case of Vladislav Tretiak during his visits to the Montreal Forum, they would be loudly cheered.

In Canada, Glasnost started with the Summit Series.

Still in 1972. Who remembers the New York Raiders and the Philadelphia Blazers? Or who remembers the first great NHL star to sign a contract with a team in the new World Hockey Association? Does Bernard Parent and Miami's Screaming Eagles ring a bell?

While the NHL was cavorting with the Soviets, Gary Davidson, a California lawyer, founded the WHA. In Winnipeg, Ben Hatskin convinced his partners and the other WHA teams to pay $1 million cash to Chicago Blackhawks superstar Bobby Hull. In Quebec, Marius Fortier

Above: Scotty Bowman grimaces behind the Team Canada bench. With a Canada Cup victory in 1976, and the most victories in NHL coaching history, Bowman's legend is well established. Known as a disciplinarian and master motivator, he has often had strained relations with his players but always manages to get maximum effort from his teams.

got Jean-Claude Tremblay from the Montreal Canadiens and the cursed league was born.

For the first time, NHL players had leverage for negotiations—and they took advantage of it. Gerry Cheevers left Boston for the Cleveland Crusaders. Teammate Derek Sanderson headed off to the Philadelphia Blazers in a chauffeur-driven limousine. The war between the NHL and the WHA had been declared.

It was to go on for seven seasons. While the teams fought for players and markets, ferocious negotiations were being held behind the scenes— sometimes even behind the back of NHL President Clarence Campbell. During those crazy years that would end in another "expansion"—this one originating in the death of the WHA and the shifting of the Hartford Whalers, Quebec Nordiques, Winnipeg Jets, and Edmonton Oilers into the NHL—teams were created, moved, and dissolved, according to the whims of businessmen.

The WHA would nevertheless contribute to these spectacular years, providing hockey with wonderful players. The Birmingham Bulls became the Baby Bulls and their young teenagers, Rick Vaive, Rob Ramage, Michel Goulet, Ken Linseman, and others would pursue brilliant careers in the National Hockey League. Also, history will record that Wayne Gretzky started his career with the Indianapolis Racers before being "sold" to the Edmonton Oilers by Nelson Skalbania.

It's obviously very personal, but my favorite WHA story concerns Gordie Howe and his two sons. Even if the WHA did nothing more than allow a 45-year-old man to play with both his sons in a major professional hockey league, it would have justified its existence.

Gordie was so happy when I met up with him in Quebec during a visit by the Houston Aeros that I realized that money and glory had taken a secondary role in his decision to come back to play. He was in the dressing room with his sons, joking around with them, but come evening on the ice, he became an eagle defending his chicks. Any opponent who tried to take advantage of the young Howes would have to account to the old man.

At the end of his first season with the Aeros, I asked Howe what had been the most difficult time of the year.

Gordie Howe with his sons, Mark and Marty.

He thought about it for a while before answering with a mischievous smile:

> During our first road trip. I waited up until one o'clock in the morning for the call from Bill Dineen, the coach, to confirm that I'd made curfew. The next morning, I asked him why he hadn't bothered to make sure the players were in their rooms. 'But I did,' he said. 'Come on Gordie, I wasn't going to call you!' I told him that I was a player like any other and that I should be the first one to keep an eye on. The older guys often are the least manageable.

Unfortunately, market forces are unforgiving. Of the four cities that gained access to the NHL through the WHA, only one still has its team: Edmonton. The Nordiques moved to Denver, Colorado; the Whalers to North Carolina; and the Winnipeg Jets became the Phoenix Coyotes.

By the end of the century, 20 years after the merger, the teams from the defunct WHA had won six Stanley Cups.

"Only Jesus saves more than Bernie!" flashed the home-made signs hanging from the walls in the Philadelphia Spectrum.

All season long, the Flyers beat their adversaries into submission on the road to the Stanley Cup finals. The team was young, made up of amazing forwards like Bobby Clarke, Rick MacLeish, and Bill Barber, all 50- to 100-point scorers. The defense, with Ed Van Impe, André "Moose" Dupont and the Watson brothers, Jim and Joe, was rugged. Mostly though, the Flyers were Bernie Parent in front of the net, and coach Fred Shero behind the bench.

The Flyers won only two Stanley Cups but captured the imagination of fans as if they had won ten. And 25 years later, the Broad Street Bullies are still very much alive in fans' memories.

Their reputation is to hockey what the Huns were to European history— devastators of all that came before them. Yet heaven alone knows what a fine team this was. The first signs appeared in 1972–73 when the Flyers finished second to Chicago in the Western Division with 85 points. Rick MacLeish had scored 50 goals on his way to 100 points while captain Bobby Clarke finished second behind Phil Esposito among NHL scorers.

Flyers defenseman André "Moose" Dupont, named after his charging hits, tangles with a Minnesota North Stars player. Bench-clearing brawls were a routine part of the "Broad Street Bullies" reign of terror during the mid-1970s.

Above: Moose Dupont gets a taste of his own medicine as he is tackled into the boards by a Montreal defender.

Right: Reggie Leach is stopped by Soviet goalie Vladislav Tretiak during an exhibition game.

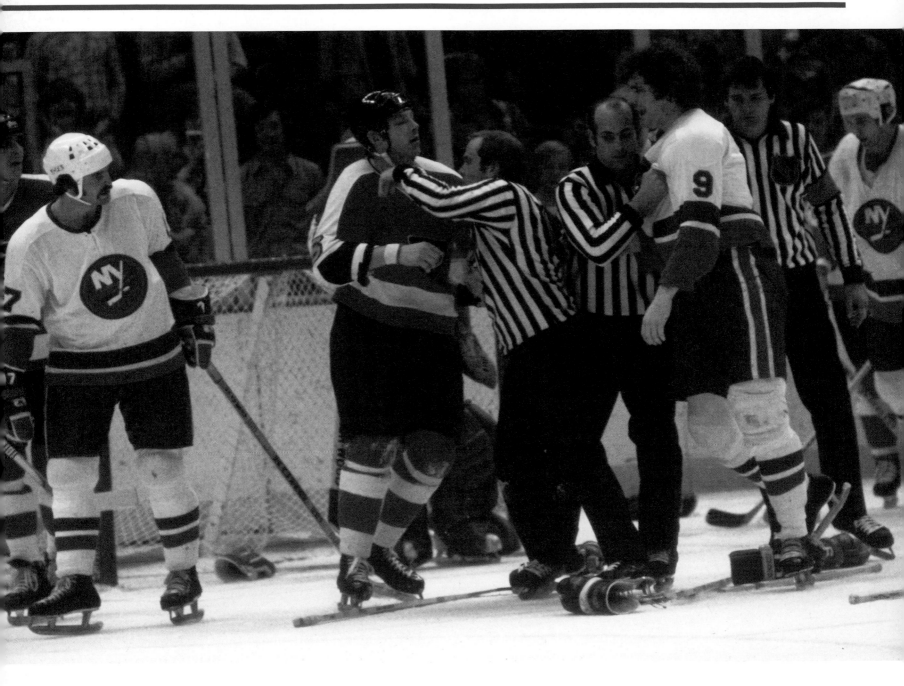

Above: Neither one willing to back down, Moose Dupont and Clark Gillies are separated by the linesman during a game between the Flyers and the Islanders.

Opposite: The ultimate "Broad Street Bully," Dave Schultz was the team's enforcer and set a single-season penalty mark of 472 minutes. Schultz's presence was relied on to deter opposing players from engaging Flyers stars like Bobby Clarke.

Opposite: One of the best to ever play the position, Bernie Parent was in nets for both Philadelphia championships in the 1970s and won the Conn Smythe Trophy on both occasions. Though he spent almost his entire career with the Flyers, Parent played briefly with the Philadelphia Blazers of the WHA after the team he signed with, The Miami Screaming Eagles, folded before the league was launched.

Clarke was an inspired leader. With his movie-star curls, piercing eyes, and innate toughness, he was the perfect captain for an expansion team lead by a coach unlike all others.

Known for his tinted glasses and legendary eccentricities, Fred "The Fog" Shero had the image of an understanding yet absent-minded father. Clarke was the leader of the pack, always the first in a fight, always the last to leave the battle.

Shero devised a game plan based on 16 points—basic elements that every player could easily comprehend. He never made long speeches; he just constantly repeated the system's 16 points.

Shero could count on an incredible goalie, one of the best in history during the Flyers' heydays, as well as on young and fearless scorers.

He could also depend on Schultz's Army to intimidate its adversaries while whipping the Spectrum crowd into a frenzy. They were four: Dave Schultz, a mild-mannered, moustached man in everyday life and a formidable warrior on the ice; Bob "Hound Dog" Kelly, a whirlwind skater with fighting ability to match; Don "The Bird" Saleski, a tall curly-haired marauder who felt brave when surrounded by the other Broad Street Bullies but ended up spending time in purgatory with the Colorado Rockies; and André Dupont, a big defenseman who supported his teammates with moose-like charges.

The Flyers altered the face of hockey for a few years. They were so spectacular, so well-liked in Philadelphia while being much hated throughout the rest of America, that they became the model team on the CBS network during Sunday afternoon American telecasts. Hockey had become a violent theater and the actors played on a stage situated in Philadelphia.

One afternoon, while the Canadiens' bus was heading toward Oakland, Scotty Bowman was sitting at the back drawing plays on a notepad. Deep in thought, Bowman suddenly looked up and whispered: "Shero's system is not all that complicated. It's Bernie Parent, good players and intimidation!"

From that moment on, the Flyers' days at the top were numbered. Within two years, the Canadiens would replace them as the model

team of North American hockey. But America and the world did not know it yet.

Bernard Parent had always been an excellent goaltender. The Flyers' triumphs began when team owner Ed Snider decided to acquire Parent from Toronto to stop him from defecting to the Miami Screaming Eagles of the WHA. Parent arrived at the right time. He and the Flyers were made for each other.

The defining moment for Parent and the Flyers, and for the new expansion teams, came against the Big Bad Bruins in the 1974 Stanley Cup finals. The top four scorers in the league wore Bruins' jerseys—Esposito, Orr, Hodge, and Cashman. Clarke came next. But those who were dazzled by Boston's reputation should have known better. The Bruins had amassed 113 points in the regular season, but that gave them only a one-point advantage over the Flyers.

The finals were typical—hard fought and occasionally brutal. Parent made the difference.

He had Jacques Plante's style, always remaining standing until the last millisecond and relying on tiger-like reflexes. At the very end, the Flyers won in Philadelphia, thanks to a goal scored by MacLeish, Dupont then performed an un-moose-like euphoric victory dance.

The stigma of expansion was a thing of the past. One of the first six expansion teams had won the Stanley Cup.

The Flyers repeated the feat the following season. They remained a close-knit family on and off the ice, the players sticking together at all times and their wives volunteering for charity work together. Their slogan was that of the Three Musketeers: "All for one and one for all!"

They continued to mix talent and intimidation, and opposing players visiting the Spectrum needed to muster their courage. There was so much talk about the "Philadelphia Flu" that some opponents dreaded a road trip to Philadelphia.

Pierre Larouche, 50-goal scorer with both the Pittsburgh Penguins and Montreal Canadiens, used to relate this anecdote: "I was getting set for a face-off in the Flyers' zone. Bobby Clarke looked at me with his fierce glare and growled: 'If you touch the puck, we'll smash your head in.' I told him, 'No problem Bobby. Take the face-off.'"

But the only way to defeat the Flyers at hockey was to defeat them in a brawl, and on two pivotal occasions, the Canadiens did just that. The second occurred one Sunday afternoon when defenseman Larry Robinson, who had gone to the dressing room to repair his skates in the dying seconds of the period, heard on the radio that a bench-clearing brawl had broken out.

He tugged his skates back on and charged back onto the ice to find Dave Schultz circling the melee looking for a partner. That was unfortunate for Schultz. Robinson pounded out a solid, one-sided decision and the Flyers were on the decline.

Perhaps it was just as well. On another Sunday afternoon, in a game against the famous Soviet Central Red Army team, the Flyers precipitated an international incident. Ed Van Impe elbowed Valeri Kharlamov, the great Russian star, so powerfully that Kharlamov went down like a sack of sand. The Soviet leaders threatened to pull their team out of the competition, and only after Alan Eagleson's intervention was the game allowed to resume.

The Flyers won, but their decline had begun.

While the Broad Street Bullies were crunching the Soviets, Parent was recuperating from a chronic injury at the Holiday Inn in Montego Bay, Jamaica. There were no satellite dishes at that time and Parent had spent the afternoon with a Montreal newspaper reporter who called the office every half-hour for news of the game.

Rest and sunshine were insufficient and Parent had to relinquish his position to Wayne Stephenson for the 1976 final against the Canadiens.

The Flyers were eliminated in four games.

No team has dominated its sport as strongly as the Montreal Canadiens did during the '50s, '60s and '70s. In the '50s their roster included Maurice Rocket Richard, Bernard Geoffrion, Dickie Moore, Doug Harvey, Jacques Plante, and company. In the '60s, led by Toe Blake, the team boasted Jean Beliveau, Henri Richard, Yvan Cournoyer, Gilles

Following pages:
Bob Gainey showers fellow Hall of Famer Bernie Parent with snow as he tries to knock a loose puck past the Philadelphia netminder.

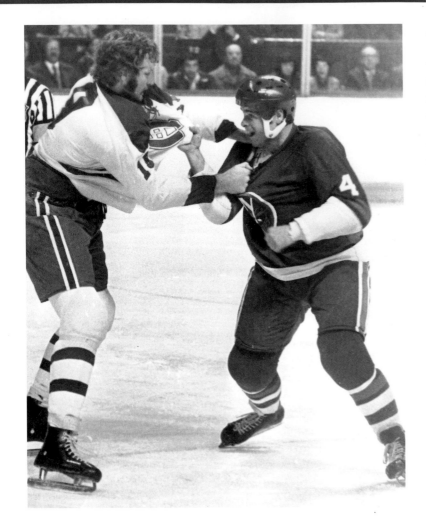

Larry Robinson squares off with Jean Potvin of the New York Islanders. Robinson was a key part of a Canadiens defensive corps that combined great hockey skill with physical toughness.

Tremblay, Jacques Laperrière, and Jean-Claude Tremblay. And before his retirement in 1978, Sam Pollock would succeed in building another dynasty, the last for this famous organization. The one from the '70s would go on to win four consecutive Stanley Cups. It was made up of great names like Guy Lafleur, Ken Dryden, Pete Mahovlich, Steve Shutt, Jacques Lemaire, and Bob Gainey, and a trio of defensemen that was without doubt the best in history—Larry Robinson, Serge Savard, and Guy Lapointe. And there was also an extraordinary coach, Scotty Bowman.

Scotty had seen it correctly. The Flyers' "system" included a good dose of intimidation. The Montreal Canadiens would first have to send the clear message that they would never be intimidated by the Broad Street Bullies.

It should have been a pre-season game like the others, tough but within the limits. There were only a few minutes left in the game when Scotty's long-awaited moment came. He had his crunch crew on the ice: Rick Chartraw, Sean Shanahan, Pierre Bouchard, Larry Robinson, good players but tough. The game turned into a monumental bench-clearing brawl. And at the end, when the reporters tallied up the results of the fights, it was evident that the Canadiens came out on top: "Now that we've showed them we are not afraid of them, we can play hockey!" declared Guy Lafleur.

He was right.

So began a fabulous adventure. It was a great team, above all a group of individuals fascinating to know and to follow. Not only did Lafleur, Lemaire, Savard, Robinson, Gainey, Dryden, and all the others win four consecutive Stanley Cups, six in all throughout the decade, but they were also the heart of the Team Canada that won the first Canada Cup in 1976.

In the 1976–77 season, the Canadiens won 60 games, earned 132 points and lost only eight games: "We'll lose fewer games in one season than the Expos lose in one week!" boasted Serge Savard before the start of the baseball season.

This team did not take well to losing, pushed by a coach who was always hard to deal with. Never has a winning team been so superior and yet still been forced to play in such a state of tension. Bowman was challenged but respected, hated but obeyed. He knew he had to control strong-willed individuals, stars with glowing personalities, men able to think and defend an opinion. He knew he had to sacrifice the egos of some for the good of the team. He got there without compromising, even if he had to live alone among members of a team acclaimed everywhere.

Generally, Bowman looked for challenges to ignite his charges. One afternoon, he was immersed in the sports pages of a Los Angeles newspaper and frantically calculating statistics. Suddenly his face became tense: "These bums, no way to get ahead of them, they won again yesterday!"

But what could he be talking about? The Canadiens were totally dominating the overall standings of the NHL. No other team should have worried him.

"It's the Denver Nuggets! They are playing .800 and were only playing .790!"

Bowman was chasing the Denver Nuggets of the American Basketball Association, a second-rate league that is now long-deceased!

The Canadiens of that era were a team different from all other teams. Later, the Islanders would blossom into a formidable dynasty with Denis Potvin, Mike Bossy, and Bryan Trottier; the Oilers would become probably the best team of all time with Wayne Gretzky, Mark Messier, and the others. But these teams could not boast a goaltender who would become a great writer like Ken Dryden or a financier involved in the politics and finances of his province like Serge Savard.

Dryden also became president of the Toronto Maple Leafs. Savard was general manager of the Canadiens for 13 years. Bob Gainey is president and general manager of the Dallas Stars. Jacques Lemaire was

Cruising behind the net, Lafleur
gathers speed as a Buffalo Sabre
vainly tries to slow his progress.

the coach of the New Jersey Devils before becoming the assistant to Canadiens general manager Réjean Houle, another name from the glory years. Larry Robinson was the coach of the Los Angeles Kings. Guy Lapointe was assistant coach with the Nordiques and now scouts for the Calgary Flames. Doug Jarvis is an assistant coach in Dallas. Steve Shutt was assistant coach with the Canadiens. Doug Risebrough was general manager of the Calgary Flames and became assistant general manager to Glen Sather of the Edmonton Oilers, another graduate of the '70s Canadiens. Yvan Cournoyer was coach Mario Tremblay's assistant in Montreal. Jim Roberts is assistant coach with the St. Louis Blues and also coached several teams in the NHL. Every one of these men agreed to follow the rules to win. Scotty's rules.

From a technical point of view, Ken Dryden was not the best goaltender. He was often off balance, and he became awkward as soon as he moved away from the net. But Dryden was rock-solid when it mattered. He might allow an easy goal in the second or third period when the Canadiens held a good lead, but he might have stopped 18 shots in the first 20 minutes when the outcome was still in doubt. When they absolutely needed to be stopped, he stopped them.

On planes, Dryden always had his nose in a book—never fiction. His teammates constantly teased him, but there was a lot of respect in their jokes. Savard was the financial adviser and his teammates depended on him for their holdings and investments. At 30, Savard was already at the helm of a fortune acquired through business deals, not from hockey. One did not become a millionaire from hockey in the '70s. Collusion between Alan Eagleson, the most powerful man in '70s hockey, and the team owners kept the salaries at a relatively modest level. A few years would go by before the earnings of the best players reached six figures.

Guy Lafleur and Jacques Lemaire used to sit in the back of the plane drinking Tia Maria and milk while discussing hockey—Lafleur out of passion, Lemaire out of fascination. Lafleur effervesced, Lemaire dissected. One had the soul of a poet, the other the soul of a coach.

"The Flower" is without a doubt the player who came nearest to Maurice Richard. He was dazzling, ardent, instinctive, and creative,

Salming jousts with an Atlanta Flames forward as the puck flies over the net.

a competitor who lived for hockey. On game day, he would get to the arena by three in the afternoon to soak up the atmosphere of the dressing room, experiencing in advance the wonderful emotions of the evening.

He was dazzling on the ice and flamboyant off it. He smoked and enjoyed cognac and champagne. He was a well-known jet-setter. He drove a Ferrari and sometimes had major car crashes. But people always loved him, always understood him, and let him live at one hundred miles an hour.

He and Bobby Orr were the players of the '70s.

Lafleur and the powerful Montreal offense filled arenas and made headlines. But in sports, it's often defense that wins championships.

And never has professional hockey known a defensive trio like The Big Three: Serge Savard, also known as "The Senator"; Guy Lapointe, known as "Pointu" after a Quebec TV character; and Larry Robinson, known as "Big Bird"—6 feet, 3 inches and 220 pounds. Most of all, they were fast and strong, and they possessed an exceptional hockey sense. All three.

Night after night, game after game, these three men would repel the opposition and launch a murderous attack. Lapointe and Robinson played together, and Savard could adapt to whomever he was paired with. In the best years, it was Bill Nyrop, who later died from cancer after becoming the owner of the West Palm Beach team in the Florida Sunshine League. The fifth defenseman was big Pierre Bouchard, a refined, cultured man in private life and a rugged enforcer in professional life.

Even the writers who covered the Canadiens of that era are members of the Hall of Fame. Red Fisher was there for the defunct *Montreal Star*, Al Strachan for *The Gazette*, Bertrand Raymond for *Le Journal de Montréal*. And the writer for *La Presse* wrote these lines: "'Les Glorieux' of the end of the decade won four consecutive Stanley Cups. But the fourth already contained elements of the crumbling dynasty."

In 1978, the year before the fourth straight win, general manager Sam Pollock, nicknamed the Godfather, had left the organization and named his successor—Irving Grundman. Grundman was one of the great gentlemen in the Canadiens, history but an outsider in the minds of the traditionalists. Scotty Bowman didn't recognize his authority and the 1978–79 season was bumpy. There were no huge storms, but there was none of the bright sunshine that had lit up the previous seasons.

The Canadiens won the Cup. But in the end, Bowman left the team to become general manager and coach for the Buffalo Sabres. Dryden announced his retirement. Lemaire left Canada to become a player-coach in Sierre, Switzerland. The Canadiens would never be the same again.

Arnie Brown of the Rangers tries to check Orr as he circles
behind the net. The most dominant defenseman ever
to play the game, Orr had no fear of joining the offensive
rush, yet was rarely caught out of position on defense.

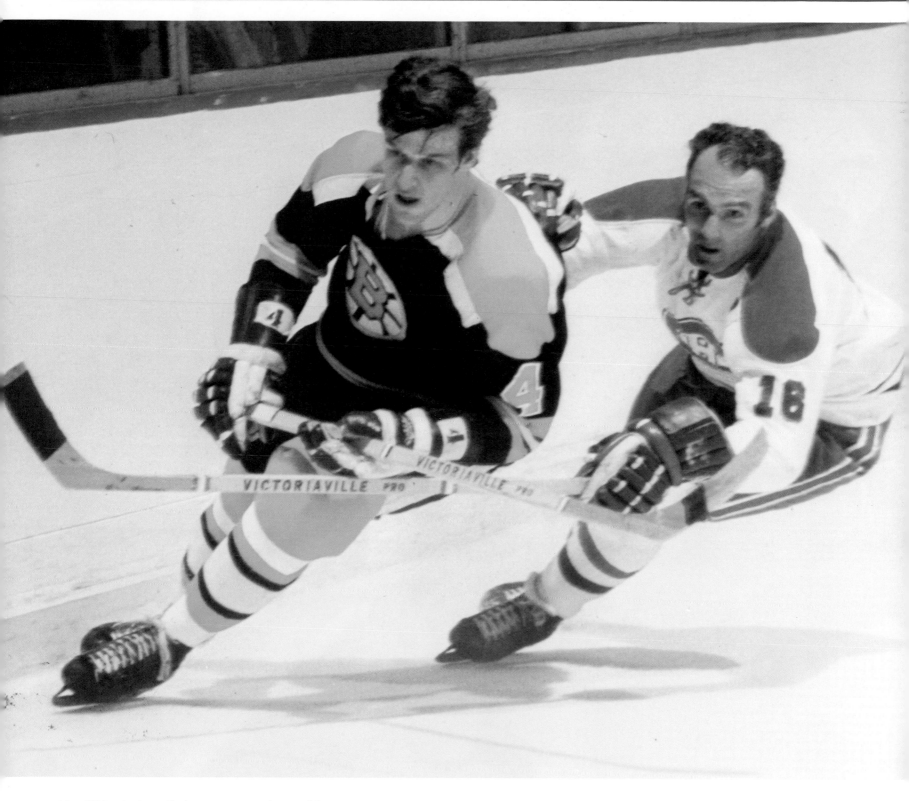

Henri Richard mirrors Orr's every move as the two follow the puck out from behind the net. The Big Bad Bruins of the '70s clashed frequently with their conference rivals from Montreal.

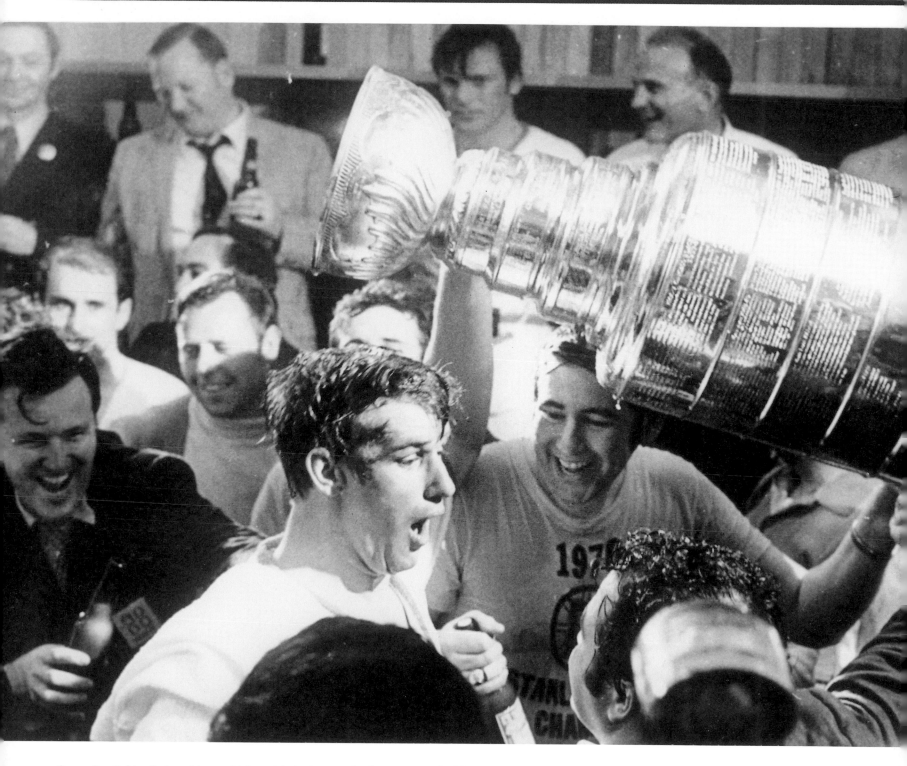

Opposite: Bobby Orr's problems with knee injuries began in his first season in the NHL. While his incredible speed and puck control allowed him to miss many collisions, it was his fearlessness that set him apart. Unafraid to charge along the boards and leap past opposing checkers, Orr was usually successful in beating opposing defenders, but not always. Often slower players caught off guard would react instinctively and stick out their knees as Orr flew past. Sometimes he could be caught in mid-air by a well-timed check along the boards. Eventually the knee injuries caught up with Orr, forcing him to sit out the 1972 Summit Series and limiting him to only 26 games in the last three years of his career before his eventual retirement in 1978.

Above: Orr takes a champagne shower as he celebrates with teammates in the Bruins dressing room after scoring the winning goal in the Finals.

Opposite: Bobby Orr keeps close to Lanny McDonald behind the Bruins net. Drafted by the Leafs in 1973 he would play seven seasons in Toronto before being traded to the Colorado Rockies in 1979. Always a fan favorite, the highlight of his career in Toronto was an overtime goal in the seventh game of the 1978 quarter-finals, against the New York Islanders. The Leafs would not win the Cup that year and McDonald wouldn't win one until the 1988–89 season, the year he retired as a Calgary Flame.

Above: Lanny McDonald and Ken Dryden captured together in a 1970s Montreal/Toronto game.

Jacques Plante played with the Maple Leafs, in the early 1970s, after Terry Sawchuk was the first goalie taken in the 1967 expansion draft, by the Los Angeles Kings.

Opposite: Darryl Sittler, one of the greatest Leafs of the expansion era, jumps to screen the Canadiens goalie. Sittler is the Maple Leafs' all-time scoring leader. Although he led the Leafs to the semifinals in 1978, he is best remembered for scoring an NHL-record 10 points in a game. On February 7, 1976, Sittler scored six goals and added four assists to set an NHL single game scoring mark that still hasn't been broken.

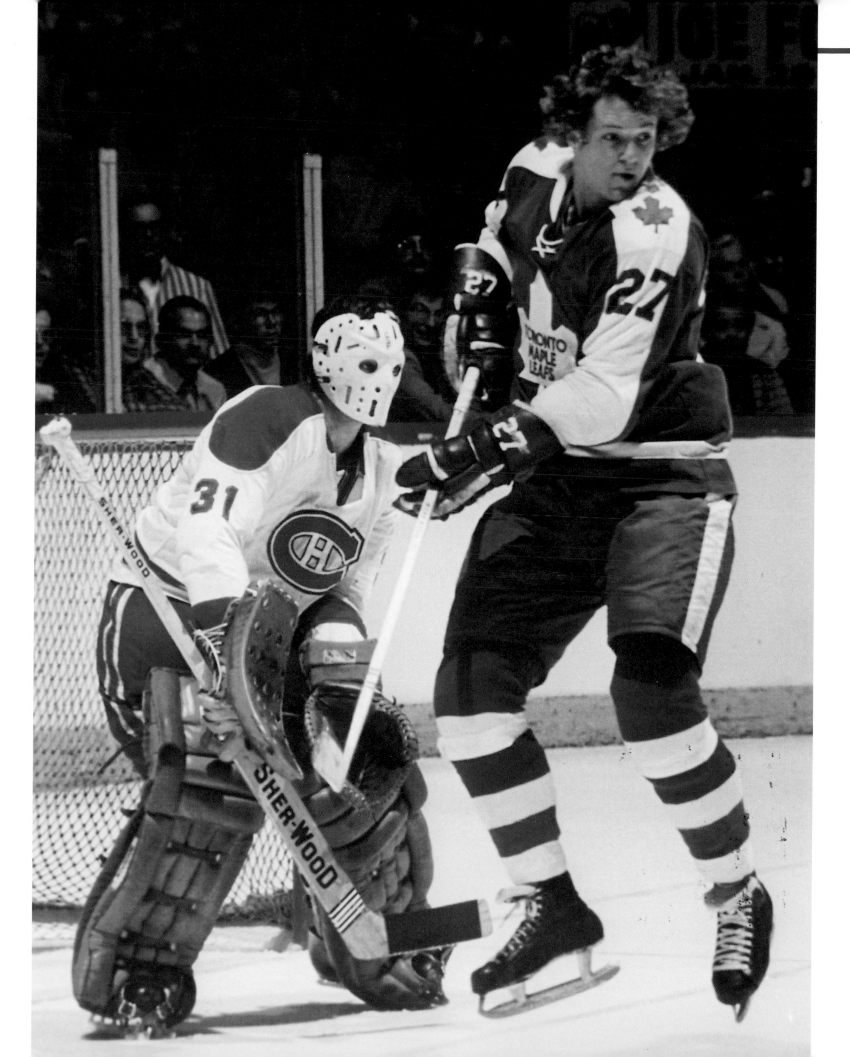

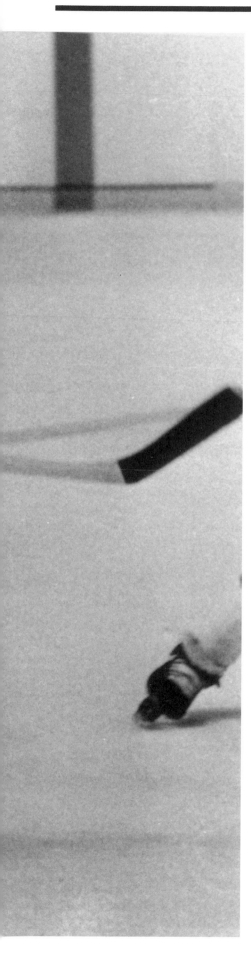

Opposite: Guy Lafleur is one of the best right-wingers ever to play the game. A charismatic character on and off the ice, everything he did was done with a sense of style. He was a vital part of five Canadiens Stanley Cups, including four in a row in the 1970s.

Above: With his flowing locks and blazing speed, a Guy Lafleur rush was one of the most exciting spectacles in hockey history.

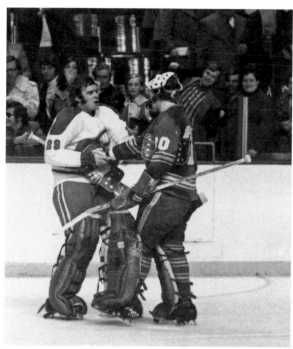

Opposite: At 6'3" Dryden was a large goalie. Rather than let this be an obstacle Dryden used his size and reach to make life difficult for opposing players. He won the Vezina Trophy trophy five times in his seven full NHL seasons and retired with the best winning percentage in the league's history.

Top: Montreal goalie Ken Dryden made an immediate impact upon arriving at the NHL. Joining the team late in the 1970–71 season he led the Canadiens to a Stanley Cup victory and won the Conn Smythe Trophy in the process. In the 1972 summit series Dryden shared the goaltending responsibilities with Tony Esposito and then won another Cup with the Habs in 1973. He sat out a year over a contractual dispute, using the time to finish his law degree. Dryden returned to the Canadiens in 1974 and won the Stanley Cup four more times between 1976 and 1979, when he retired after only seven full NHL seasons.

Above: Brothers Dave and Ken Dryden meet at center ice to shake hands after a hard-fought game.

Opposite: Canadiens forward Yvan Cournoyer is surrounded by black shirts as he drives to the front of the Bruins net.

Top: The younger and smaller brother of Maurice "the Rocket" Richard, Henri Richard inevitably earned the moniker "Pocket Rocket." He played 20 seasons for the Canadiens, winning a record 11 Stanley Cups.

Above: Jacques Lemaire was always a student of the game who in later life would coach the New Jersey Devils to a Stanley Cup victory.

Using the net as a screen, Larry Robinson tries to shake a Toronto forechecker and begin the Montreal rush.

Time has a way of taking the sheen off sporting achievements. The recurring cycle of winners and losers, combined with relentless assaults on the record book, tends to take the lustre off the highlights of previous decades. But not always.

A full 15 years after the Edmonton Oilers won their first Stanley Cup, Glen Sather was still in awe of the team that dominated the National Hockey League in the '80s.

Sather coached that team. He was also its primary builder. Since 1980, he has been the Oilers' general manager, and when he reminisced about those early days in a 1999 interview, he did so with the fondness of an old man recalling his first love.

"Those guys all seemed to collectively develop together," he remembered.

They grew up together. I didn't find any problems handling them. They were like a bunch of young thoroughbreds. They were always kicking their heels up and ready to go. They loved to play. I knew at the time that they were going to be a part of hockey history. I think they did too. That's why we didn't have many petty jealousies on that team. They were all playing together and playing to win. They were like a family. I don't know if you're going to get that anymore, but in those days they were a big happy family.

The NHL had never seen a team like that before. Perhaps it never will again. The Oilers not only dominated the decade, winning five Stanley Cups in seven years, they may be responsible for creating hockey as we know it.

Even though the NHL had seen other dynasties, including the one forged by the New York Islanders that prevailed in the first part of the decade, hockey was not in good shape at the time. And that's a charitable view.

The product itself was generally abysmal. Artistry was scarce but

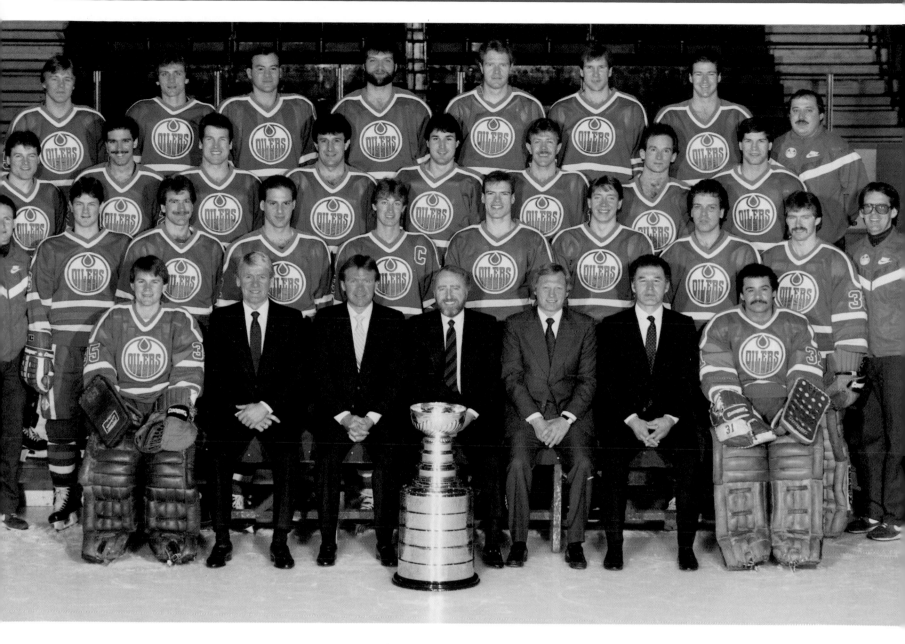

A team shot of the young Oilers and
the Stanley Cup in 1984.

Gretzky carries the puck
in on his backhand.

bench-clearing brawls were frequent. Stick-swinging duels were not uncommon. Games routinely dragged past the three-hour mark thanks to fights, post-whistle scrums, and other needless stoppages. The balanced schedule placed significant travel strains on the players and prevented the emergence of any real rivalries. The strong teams were indeed strong, but the weak teams were laughable, as much as 81 points out of first place.

Off the ice, the situation was just as bad. There was no network television in the United States. The recently concluded bitter struggle with the World Hockey Association had created huge rifts among the NHL owners, and the league spent more time dealing with court cases than with the game.

This was the sorry scene onto which the young Oilers burst. Led by the incomparable Wayne Gretzky, they dazzled hockey fans with their flair, speed, creativity, and effervescence. For years, hockey talk had centered on what was wrong with the game. Now, suddenly and refreshingly, the debates centered on Gretzky and the Oilers.

Was Gretzky really the best player ever or was he just shining because the competition was so weak? Even though the Oilers were fun to watch, could they ever win a Stanley Cup with that style? Was this team destined for greatness or was it just a collection of cocky kids who were inevitably going to get their comeuppance?

Astonishing as it may seem now, a surprisingly large segment of the contemporary hockey world saw Gretzky and the Oilers as

Al Arbour led the Islanders to four Stanley Cup victories in the 1980s, becoming one of the most successful coaches in playoff history.

impostors. Stan Fischler, the New York hockey writer who has a sizable following, decreed that Gretzky could not have survived in the six-team league because someone like Black Jack Stewart would have wiped him out with a crunching bodycheck. In fact, Stewart couldn't even skate backwards, but it didn't really matter that Fischler and others were so astonishingly wrong. What mattered was that hockey fans were once again, after such a long hiatus, debating the game of hockey rather than the problems of hockey.

But standing between the Oilers and their place in hockey history were the New York Islanders, a team that, for a brief period, was touted as possibly the best in hockey history. Had it not been for the Oilers' emergence so soon afterwards, perhaps a strong case could have been made in that regard. Certainly the Islanders were a true powerhouse from top to bottom.

Bill Torrey was a superb general manager. Al "Radar" Arbour was an excellent coach, albeit one who had a propensity for defensive hockey which, while it pleases the purists, does not do much for the aesthetics of the game. And from Billy Smith in goal, to Denis Potvin and Stefan Persson on defence, to Mike Bossy, Bryan Trottier, and Clark Gillies up front, the Islanders were a truly dominant aggregation.

Top left:
Defenseman Stefan Persson ran the point on the Islanders' power play.

Bottom left:
Vancouver tough guy Tiger Williams, not known for his scoring touch, closes in on Billy Smith in the 1982 finals.

Right: A winner of six Stanley Cup championships during his 18 seasons in the NHL, Trottier won four straight with the New York Islanders and a pair more with Pittsburgh at the end of his career.

In 1981 they proved that point. Their first Stanley Cup, a year earlier, had left them with some doubters. The perennially powerful Montreal Canadiens, who had won the four previous Cups, had run into a rash of injuries and, missing eight regulars, including Guy Lafleur, had been upset by the Minnesota North Stars. The Islanders had finished only fifth in the season standings, but with the Canadiens out of the way and with trading-deadline acquisition Butch Goring producing a superb playoff performance, the Islanders managed to scrape past the Philadelphia Flyers, thanks, in part, to some dubious officiating. But the Islanders had to prove their worth. As expected, they had little difficulty with the Toronto Maple Leafs in the first round, but then they had to face that dynamic young Edmonton team. Though they persevered, it wasn't easy.

Against the New York Rangers, they lost Persson, a key point man on the power play, to injury. But Mike McEwen, yet another of Torrey's late-season acquisitions, filled in admirably and the Islanders' power play continued to annihilate the opposition, rolling along at a success rate of almost 30 percent.

McEwen had been picked up for Glenn Resch and Steve Tambellini on March 10, a trade that was reviled by the media. Another late arrival, Bill

Previous pages:
A scrum erupts in front of the net as Islanders defenders try to clear the pressing Canucks forwards away from their goaltender.

Top: Always dangerous, 50-goal scorer Mike Bossy aims a backhand at the Vancouver net.

Below: The Flyers' captain Bobby Clarke is greeted by Clark Gillies in front of the Islanders net.

Opposite: Butch Goring was acquired by the Islanders in 1980 and the team went on to win four Stanley Cups. A former winner of the Lady Byng Trophy (awarded to the league's most sportsmanlike player), Goring won the Conn Smythe Trophy in his second season with New York. After he retired Goring began a coaching career with the Boston Bruins and then as a minor league coach. In 1999 he returned to the NHL to coach his struggling former team, the Islanders.

Clark Gillies provided a physical presence during the Islander's dynasty of the 1980s. On a team that boasted such skilled players as Mike Bossy, Denis Potvin, and Brian Trottier, Gillies played the role of enforcer, ensuring that other teams didn't take liberties with the Islanders' stars.

Carroll, who had spent most of the year on the farm team, combined with Goring to form an elite penalty-killing unit that for one lengthy playoff stretch scored as many goals as it allowed.

The North Stars managed to push the finals to five games, but the Islanders scored 26 goals; by the time it was over, there were no longer any doubters. The Islanders were now the undisputed kings of the NHL hill. The only question that remained was how long they would stay there.

Known as a fearless goalie, Billy Smith had no qualms about leaving his net to engage opposing players.

Because Torrey had made them so powerful down the left side, their reign lasted four years. In those days, NHL teams tended to be unbalanced. The Islanders weren't. They got scoring from areas that were wastelands on other teams.

Even in the early '80s, you couldn't win Stanley Cups solely because your left wingers were better than anybody else's. But once the solid team was in place, New York's left-wingers put them over the top.

The world is predominantly right-handed, which means that most centers find it easier to pass to their right than to their left. Therefore, a disproportionate number of the league's snipers were right wingers. But on the Islanders, three of the team's regular top six scorers were left wings.

In the midst of the Islanders' dynasty, the four left wings—Gillies, John Tonelli, Bob Bourne, and Anders Kallur—averaged 30 goals a season each. Because most teams had their power on the right wing, coaches tended to install their best defensemen on the left side as a counter-measure. So the Islanders found themselves in the envious position of having their stronger forwards facing weaker defensemen.

In 1982, a series of bizarre upsets led to the 11th-place Vancouver Canucks getting to the finals, without beating a single team that finished ahead of them in the standings. The powerful Islanders had little trouble wiping them out in four games.

But by the time the following season opened, the gathering storm was on the horizon. In the eastern United States, the mighty Islanders, the seasoned veterans of the hockey wars, were looking for a fourth consecutive Cup. In western Canada, the upstart Oilers, after setting a host of single-season offensive records, were looking for the credibility that could come only with their own Cup.

In the previous season, their over-confidence had produced a stunning upset at the hands of the Los Angeles Kings, the most memorable game in the series being the one which saw the Oilers fritter away a 5–0 third-period lead to lose in overtime.

There were other contenders, but the New York and Edmonton teams were the most likely opponents in a Stanley Cup final. The Chicago Blackhawks had Denis Savard and Doug Wilson, but not the depth. The Philadelphia Flyers were perennial also-rans, as were the Boston Bruins. The Montreal Canadiens had seen their dynasty blown apart when legendary general manager Sam Pollock departed in 1978. For a while, they survived on Pollock's legacy, but when his successor Irving Grundman opened the 1982–83 season with an appalling trade, the Canadiens were out of the running for the foreseeable future.

Then, as now, elite defensemen were the most elusive commodity in the league. But Grundman shipped Rod Langway and Brian Engblom, who were arguably the two best defensemen in the league at the time, to the Washington Capitals. He even included Doug Jarvis and Craig Laughlin in the package, getting in return only Ryan Walter and Rick Green.

After a long NHL career, Trottier retired as the 15th leading goal scorer in NHL history.

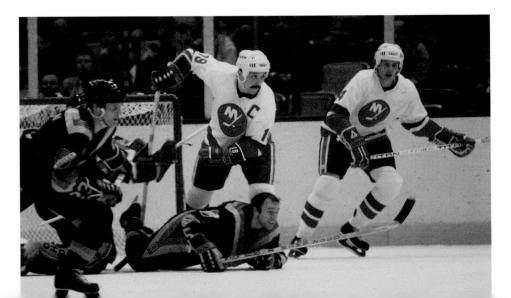

Canadiens Coach Bob Berry was so upset that he refused to show up for the press conference held to announce the trade. Publicly, he insisted that he had simply got the time wrong, but that was just a cover-up. In fact, he was furious. He heard about it on the radio, not having even been given the courtesy of a warning from Grundman that the trade was coming. Berry told friends afterwards that he stood staring at the radio, waiting for more names to be revealed. He couldn't believe that Grundman had given away so much for so little. As a result, he couldn't trust himself to say the right things at a press conference.

Grundman, who had passed up Verdun's Denis Savard for Doug Wickenheiser in the 1980 draft, was already on shaky ground. When, as expected, the Canadiens made their fourth early playoff exit in as many years, Grundman was axed.

The Oilers, meanwhile, did not repeat their embarrassment of the previous year. But they didn't win either. Although the Islanders wouldn't be able to hold on much longer, in 1983, their experience, combined with their defensive excellence, proved to be too much to handle. The result was a sweep, with the Oilers managing to score only six times in the four games.

"But that was the year we learned the lesson that enabled us to win afterwards," explained Sather.

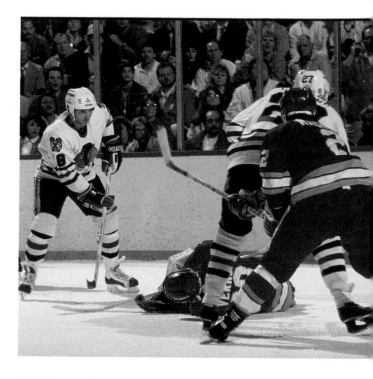

Mike Vernon of the Calgary Flames sprawls to stop a shot from the Hawks' Denis Savard.

To get out of that rink, you had to go past the Islanders' dressing room. You could look in the door and see those guys and see what their commitment was. They were cut and bruised and getting iced. It showed everybody on our team what it took to win.

The guys on our team hated losing, but at that stage, they didn't know what it took to win. After that loss to the Islanders, they did. It changed the work ethic. After that, you'd see it in the way we practiced and in a lot of little things. On our line drills, for instance, you couldn't stop until you got there. A lot of players or teams will do end-to-end rushes and will start coasting at the red line. They wouldn't coast. They got to the point that it became automatic. They pushed themselves further and further. After a while, you didn't

Above: John Tonelli leans into a slapshot. Tonelli was one four left-wingers who, during the New York Islanders' dynasty, averaged 30 goals a season. Bob Bourne, Anders Kallur, and Clark Gillies were the others.

Right: Anders Kallur

Opposite: Bob Bourne added offensive punch to the powerful Islanders lineup.

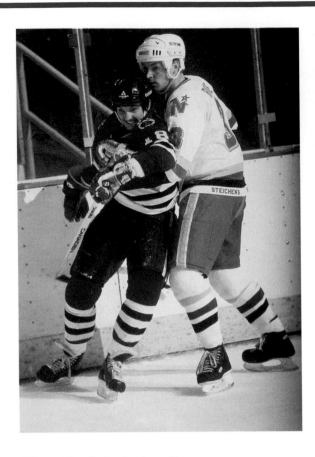

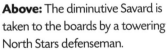

Above: The diminutive Savard is taken to the boards by a towering North Stars defenseman.

Above right: Denis Savard of the Blackhawks fires a shot past an Islanders' defender.

have to say anything. They knew what it took to win and the Islanders did that other part of teaching them what it took to win.

The Islanders' won their fourth Cup in 1983, and it was to be their last. Changes were in store for the National Hockey League—and not just in the area of on-ice domination. Canada's role in the league was about to enter a momentous phase. The next seven Stanley Cups were to be won by Canadian-based teams, an era of dominance that will probably never be repeated. Yet at the same time, the seeds were being sown for the deterioration of Canada's role in what the country sees as its national game.

It was in 1983 that the Winnipeg Jets began receiving offers from cities willing to take them should they need to relocate, which seemed likely. Eleven days after the Islanders won the Cup, the NHL's board of governors, by a 15–3 vote, turned down a bid by Saskatoon interests to buy the St. Louis Blues. The governors made it clear that they had not the slightest interest in adding any more franchises in Canada, a decision that was not particularly surprising in view of the fact that Canadian teams tended to be such poor box-office draws in the United States.

Of the NHL's eight worst road draws in the 1983–84 season, four were based in Canada. Three of the others were non-playoff teams. Apparently, as far as American fans were concerned, Canadian teams and bad teams evoked roughly the same degree of interest. It was into this climate that Hamilton's Copps Coliseum was born. The city's mayor, Bob Morrow, boldly decreed that his was "a city which will have its own NHL franchise." Evidently, he had not discussed the matter with any NHL governors.

Since the NHL has no gate-sharing provisions, the American owners couldn't have cared less about Hamilton's support for a team. They didn't want any more of those bad Canadian draws coming into their buildings. The only Canadian team they were really pleased to see was the Oilers. With Gretzky being the talk of the hockey world by that time, the Oilers were the league's best road draw.

Gretzky's regular-season performance had been nothing short of phenomenal. In the middle of the 1980–81 season, Phil Esposito retired. By the end of the 1981–82 season, Gretzky had shattered Espo's record of 76 goals in a season by scoring 92. By the standards Gretzky was later to set, it was a relatively poor performance—"only" 164 points. Even so, he broke the NHL's point-scoring record by 12 points. It turned out to be the eighth-best total of his career. By the 1985–86 season, he was up to 215 points, a record that still stands. That was the year he had 163 regular season assists, also an NHL record.

In the five seasons beginning in 1981–82, Gretzky racked up the incredible total of 1036 points. By 1989, when he broke Gordie Howe's all-time record of 1850 points after only 10 seasons, he had altered the face of hockey, just as Babe Ruth altered the face of baseball. Before Gretzky, no one had ever averaged as much as 1.4 points per game. Gretzky's average was 2.37, almost a full point a game better that the

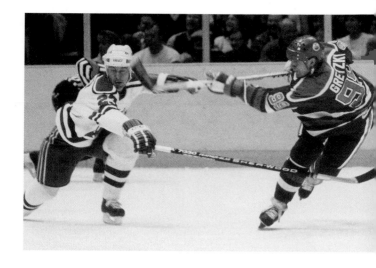

Gretzky blasts a slapshot as a Devil tries to deflect the puck.

Islanders goalie Kelly Hindy makes a stop on an airborne Montreal Canadian.

best hockey had ever seen. As often as not throughout the '80s, Gretzky's assists alone were enough to earn him the scoring title, even though he averaged more than 60 goals a season.

Still, by 1984, the Oilers had not won a Stanley Cup and there was no shortage of detractors who said they never would. The flashy five-goals-a-game average was fine for the regular season, they insisted, but it would never withstand the crunch of playoff hockey.

The two opposing views came face to face in 1984, a rematch of the previous year that pitted the veteran Islanders against the high-flying Oilers. In their 10 previous meetings, the Oilers had lost all 10. But this time, they were ready.

They remembered how battered the Islanders had been at the end of the previous year's series and this time, they didn't give an inch. They had a nine-day break before the finals, thanks to a sweep of the North Stars, and they spent much of it doing something they rarely did—studying videotapes.

They watched the way the Islanders had fore-checked the New York Rangers to a standstill in the divisional semi-finals. They watched the defensive excellence they had shown against the Montreal Canadiens in the conference final. They also looked at some year-old tapes and saw themselves being humiliated.

The fact that the Islanders were a veteran team was an advantage in many ways. But Sather kept repeating to his players that the Islanders were like old dogs. They weren't going to learn any new tricks.

So when the series began, the Oilers were well prepared. Even though they loved to break out up the middle, they knew that the Islanders expected that and were capable of producing turnovers. So they used other methods. They stuck with the pressure offense they loved so much but they combined it with the approach that Sather had noticed them developing in practice. They never eased off. If the Islanders got control in their own end, the Oilers raced back to the defensive positions with all the enthusiasm they had shown on offense.

As a result, there were no more prolonged sieges of Grant Fuhr in the Edmonton net. There were no moments of respite for the weary, battle-ravaged Islanders, and this was crucial. The Oilers arrived at the finals via 14 games against relatively easy opposition. The Islanders had 16 games against three tough teams. Ken Morrow was nursing a bad knee. Potvin had back problems. Dave Langevin and Persson were limited by shoulder injuries. And to top it off, goaltender Billy Smith was producing his first ordinary playoffs in recent memory. Normally, his playoff performances varied from incredible to miraculous.

When it was over, there was no doubt as to which was the better team. The Oilers set the tone by winning the opener 1–0 in Nassau County Coliseum, then won the series in five games with further victories of 7–2, 7–2 and 5–2.

Grant Fuhr makes a kick save on a low shot. The acrobatic goalie was an integral part of Edmonton's four Cups in the 1980s.

Reminiscing about it a few years later, Gretzky said,

I remember on our plane coming back after we lost. All our guys were pretty healthy and in good shape. We said, "They're hurting right now and we're not. That was the difference." To be brave in hockey is driving to the net and standing in front of the net and getting deflections. That's what brave is. That's what the Islanders did to us. You have to pay the price. The next year, we did that. That was the big difference.

It was the first of the Oilers' five Cups in seven years. And perhaps it was the most rewarding. If not, then the last one would be. On those two occasions, there was some doubt as to whether the Oilers would win. For the rest of the decade, except for a few brief spells here and there, they were always expected to win. Sometimes they did; sometimes they didn't. But when they lost, they usually had themselves to blame.

They were the class of the league in that era and Gretzky was the dominant player. Mario Lemieux was drafted in 1984 but did hockey's image no favors by behaving petulantly at the draft. He refused to follow the custom of walking to the table to meet the staff of his new team, instead remaining in the Montreal Forum stands while his agent, Gus Badali, pushed away any mere mortal who came too close.

Approximately 4000 fans who were watching a live feed of the proceedings at the Civic Arena in Pittsburgh booed loudly. Although Lemieux would eventually blossom into one of premier players in NHL history, it was not until his fifth year that he was able to lead the Penguins into the playoffs.

The Philadelphia Flyers were also a powerful team in the '80s and turned out to be the team that the Oilers had to overcome in 1985 to earn their second successive Stanley Cup. The Oilers were flying that year and rolled to the Cup with only three losses. One of them was the opener of the finals, but after that, they had no real difficulties.

In their hearts, Flyers fans had anticipated such a result, but had hoped that their team would continue to improve and perhaps get their own back the following season. But that November, the death of goal-

A young Mario Lemieux was drafted by the Pittsburgh Penguins and went on to lead them to two Stanley Cups during his illustrious career. Lemieux has now re-emerged on the hockey scene as a potential buyer for the financially bankrupt Pittsburgh club.

Pelle Lindbergh, a native of Sweden, was drafted by the Flyers in 1979. He went on to become an NHL star in the early '80s, winning the Vezina Trophy in 1985. He died tragically in a single-car accident in 1985.

tender Pelle Lindbergh in a car accident dealt them, and all of hockey, a terrible blow.

In a memorial service at the Spectrum prior to the Flyers' next home game, former Philly star Bernie Parent, Lindbergh's mentor and close friend, brought tears to the fans' eyes and to his own. "No single moment in my hockey career has been as difficult as this one," he said. "The paper has said I was his hero. I wish I could tell you how much I admired him, how much I cared about him. When death defeats greatness, we all mourn. When death defeats youth, we mourn even more."

Lindbergh was only one of many great European stars who made an impact on the NHL in the '80s. The Swedish invasion was well under way by that time, but there were also moves afoot to make the NHL what it is today, a true world all-star league.

To do that, a way had to be found to get players out from behind the Iron Curtain. The Czechoslovaks had made their mark in the 1976 Canada Cup, but it was the Russians that North Americans really wanted to see.

There was a mystique about them, one that was perpetuated every time they faced NHL competition. They were the yardstick by which international success was measured, and one of the defining moments in the development of hockey in the United States occurred early in the decade—Feb. 22, 1980, to be exact. In what became known as "The Miracle on Ice," the Americans defeated the mighty Soviet Union team at the Lake Placid Olympics.

It's often forgotten that it was not a gold-medal game; it was the opener of the medal round. But the United States was given no chance,

Pelle Lindbergh prepares to pounce on a loose puck in front of his net.

Team USA players flood onto the ice after they upset the powerhouse Soviet Union in the 1980 Winter Olympics. The victory has since become known as the Miracle on Ice. The Americans would go on to capture the Gold Medal.

not only because they weren't a major hockey power but because the Soviets had won four consecutive Olympics. In a pre-Olympic exhibition game, the U.S.S.R. defeated the U.S.A. 10–3.

However, on that memorable afternoon, Jim Craig became an instant hero by making 39 saves, and the Americans, down 3–2 going into the final period, won 4–3 on goals by Mark Johnson and Mike Eruzione. Two days later, the U.S. beat Finland 4–2 to win the gold.

The Soviets certainly avenged that embarrassment in the 1981 Canada Cup when they defeated Team Canada 8–1 in the sudden-death final game. Through time, that defeat has come to represent one of Canada's darkest hours, but it wasn't really that bad.

Of Team Canada's 7 games, only the last one was a loss, and the 8–1 score wasn't representative of the play. The game was close for more than two periods, during which Soviet goaltender Vladislav Tretiak made the difference. But once the Canadians fell behind, they were forced to open up and when that happened, the Soviets' precise offensive attack tore them apart.

Not until 1989, when Sergei Priakin joined the Calgary Flames, were Soviet players released to the NHL, but the movement had begun long before that. In 1982, the NHL and the Soviet Ice Hockey Federation agreed to talk about the concept on the condition that the players did not stay in North America once their careers had ended. Sensing a move in that direction, some NHL clubs had drafted Soviet stars. The North Stars took Viktor Zhluktov and the New York Rangers picked Sergei Kapustin. The Montreal Canadiens showed astonishing prescience by selecting Viacheslav Fetisov, who did indeed turn out to be one of the first Soviets released. But it didn't happen until 1989, and he went to the New Jersey Devils, having re-entered the draft.

By late 1984, Flyers owner Ed Snider was trying to drum up support for a world championship series pitting the Soviet Union's top club team against the Stanley Cup winner. The idea never came to fruition, partly because Snider later turned against the Soviets for their treatment of Jews.

The Canada Cup series continued, though, with tournaments in 1984 and 1987. As usual, they stirred up oceans of anguish in Canada, but the

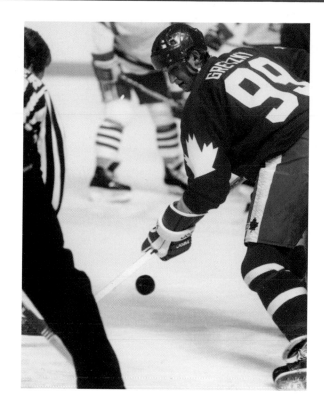

Wayne Gretzky's eyes lock on the puck as it leaves the linesman's hand during this 1984 Canada Cup face-off.

Above: Lanny McDonald, a longtime fan favorite in Toronto, spent most of the '80s as a co-captain of the Calgary Flames. McDonald finished his career in dramatic fashion, netting his 500th goal, scoring his 1000th point and winning the Stanley Cup in 1989, the year he retired.

Opposite: Joey Mullen was a major part of the strong Calgary teams of the 1980s. He was the first American player to score over 500 goals and the first to reach 1000 points.

home team won both of them, with the 1987 triumph providing some of the greatest hockey that has ever been seen.

Suddenly, in the middle of the 1989 Stanley Cup finals, a state-controlled news agency in the Soviet Union announced that Fetisov, Sergei Makarov, and Igor Larionov would be demobilized by the Red Army and join NHL teams. The Soviet players quickly learned North American ways. They hired an agent to make sure that they got all that was coming to them, and, within two weeks, Larionov had fired his first agent and hired another. One of Makarov's first actions on North American soil was to denounce his previous coach, Viktor Tikhonov, at a press conference staged by his new team, the Calgary Flames. "Tikhonov thinks he plays," he said. "It's not Tikhonov who plays. It's the team who plays. You could call him a dictator. I would still be there if Tikhonov were not the coach."

By the time the season started, the third member of the famed KLM Line, Vladimir Krutov, had been allowed to join Larionov on the Vancouver Canucks. Krutov never did pan out. In fact, the Canucks unsuccessfully filed suit to have his contract overturned. Makarov won the Calder Trophy, a development that so outraged many hockey fans that it prompted a change in qualifications. Now, only rookies under 26 are considered. After seven adequate years with three teams, Makarov returned home, but Larionov and Fetisov stayed on to win Stanley Cups with the Detroit Red Wings.

Through all this, the Oilers remained the league's powerhouse, even though they were starting to crumble from within. In 1986, they were beaten in the second round by the Calgary Flames when they forgot the principles that had led them to that first win against the Islanders.

General manager Cliff Fletcher had put together a good team in Calgary. In the spring, he added the missing links. He pried Joey Mullen out of St. Louis to give the team the sniper it so badly needed and acquired the rugged, playoff-hardened Tonelli from the Islanders. Well coached by Bob Johnson, the Flames did everything they could to take the Oilers off their game, from deliberate slowing of the play to cheap shots and scrums after every whistle.

The Oilers' coaches told their charges to forget both the pretty stuff and the petty stuff, to play a dump-and-chase style. Every time the Oilers fell behind in the series, they produced a grinding game to pull even. But it wasn't enough. After the warm-up prior to Game Seven, the Oilers listened to their coaches stress the need to dump the puck—then went the entire first period without doing it once.

In the third period, on his 23rd birthday, Edmonton defenseman Steve Smith banked the winning goal into the net off Fuhr's leg. Literally and figuratively, the Oilers had beaten themselves.

There are many who think that at any other time in hockey history, the Flames could have been a dynasty. But in this, their first of two visits to the Stanley Cup final in four years, they fell short, losing to the Montreal Canadiens, whose superb checking line of Bob Gainey, Guy Carbonneau, and Chris Nilan shut down Mullen's line. The Flames had a stretch of 198 minutes in which they couldn't score at even strength and one of 120 minutes in which they couldn't score at all.

The game plan that the Oilers refused to follow was practiced to perfection by the Canadiens, and the Flames, missing two of their best players, Gary Suter and Carey Wilson, went down in five.

But the Oilers learned their lesson—for the most part—and the next year, they were back in the finals. They should have disposed of the Philadelphia Flyers long before the seventh game, but at least this time, when they needed a strong defensive game, they produced it and came away with a 3–1 victory.

Their 1988 victory the following year was almost an anti-climax. The Oilers had slacked off in the regular

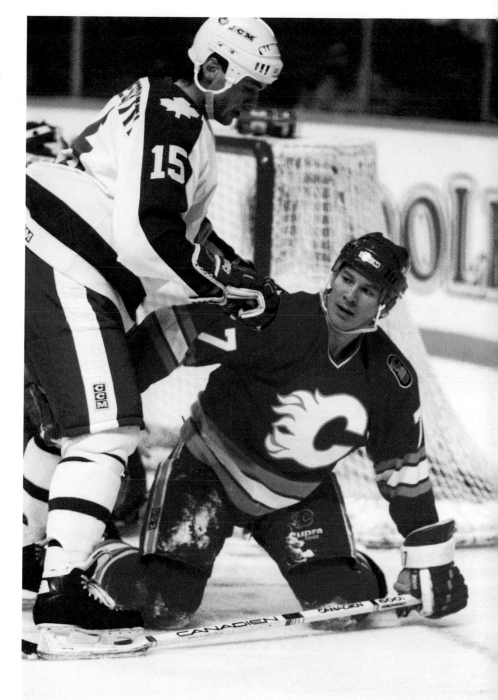

season and by the time the playoffs started, the Flames were the favorites. But the Oilers not only defeated them, they swept the series. The discipline that had been lacking two years earlier was in full evidence this time and the Flames' tactics no longer worked. The league was in the throes of one of its crackdowns, so the cheap shots earned penalties and the Flames paid the predictable price. Gretzky was brilliant and, by the time the Oilers knocked off the Boston Bruins in a series

Above: Jamie Macoun stands in to block a Claude Lemieux slapshot.

Left: Steve Smith is consoled by teammate Don Jackson after mistakenly scoring on his own net. It was Smith's rookie season in the NHL and the goal effectively eliminated the Oilers from their series against the Calgary Flames.

Opposite: Lemieux gives Calgary goaltender Mike Vernon a mask full of snow as Vernon stops a Montreal rush.

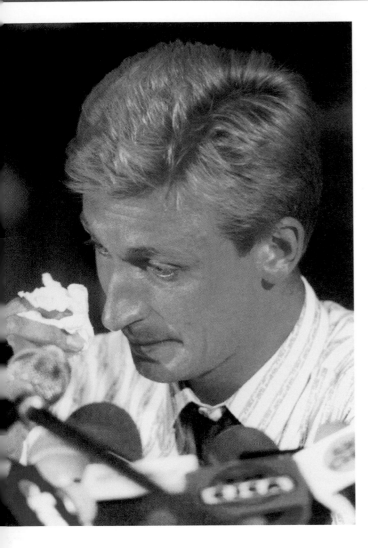

delayed by a power failure in decrepit, crumbling Boston Garden, he was a shoo-in for the Conn Smythe Trophy as the most valuable player in the playoffs.

But two months later, the hockey world was shocked when Gretzky was sold to the Los Angeles Kings for US$15 million in a deal that was made to look like a trade by the inclusion of other players. Marty McSorley and Mike Krushelnyski also went to the Kings, who sent back Martin Gelinas, Jimmy Carson, and three first-round draft picks.

It was a cash grab by Oilers owner Peter Pocklington who, for years, had been trying to keep his other business ventures afloat by taking more and more money out of the Oilers. In 1987, he had filed a proposal with the NHL board of governors whereby he would allow at least 60 percent of the team to be publicly traded. He valued the team at $100 million, having bought it in 1979 for $6.5 million.

The concept never came to fruition so Pocklington instead sold the team's major asset. After Gretzky had joined the Kings, Pocklington also offered to sell Grant Fuhr for US$5 million, then recanted, saying that it was a practical joke.

The whole episode unearthed another seamy side of the NHL. In his

Above: Wayne Gretzky is overwhelmed by emotion during the press conference announcing his famous trade to the Los Angeles Kings. Gretzky has been credited with popularizing hockey in California and facilitating the NHL's expansion into the Sun Belt.

Opposite: Grant Fuhr tries to keep his focus as former teammate and captain Wayne Gretzky lurks at the edge of his vision. In an interesting twist of fate, Gretzky would score the goal that broke Gordie Howe's scoring record in Edmonton against his former team.

Calgary's Doug Gilmour celebrates as Calgary scores on
Patrick Roy. Chris Chelios looks on helplessly.

entire career in Edmonton, Gretzky's contract had never been filed with the league. In June 1988, he was assured by his legal adviser that he had the right to declare himself a free agent. Instead, he offered to sign a new Edmonton deal with an eight-year no-trade clause.

Pocklington responded by offering him to at least four teams—the Kings, the Rangers, the Red Wings, and the Canucks. As soon as he received a phone call from Kings owner Bruce McNall explaining the situation and requesting a meeting, Gretzky decided to leave the Oilers. "Would you want to go back and play for somebody after you got a phone call from another owner?" he asked.

He was meeting with McNall just after agreeing to play in Los Angeles when the phone rang. It was Pocklington. McNall switched to the speaker phone and heard Pocklington ask whether the deal was to be made.

"Ask him for McSorley," mouthed Gretzky in McNall's direction. McNall did so, but Pocklington said he'd have to talk to Sather about that. Gretzky began waving his arms furiously. McNall excused himself and put Pocklington on hold.

"Don't let him talk to Slats," said Gretzky. "There's no way Slats will let Marty go."

McNall reconnected to Pocklington and said, "Either Marty's in or the deal is off and I have to know right now."

"Okay," said Pocklington. "He's in."

Ironically, Pocklington had just become the author of his own demise. He had been paying Gretzky $1 million a year. McNall immediately gave Gretzky an eight-year, $20 million contract. Not long afterward, he tore that one up to give Gretzky another raise. Gretzky was the industry bellwether and when he got a 150 percent increase, the price of hockey players rose accordingly across the board. This began the salary spiral that has yet to end.

With Gretzky in Los Angeles, the Kings were a motivated team when they met the Oilers in the first round of the 1989 playoffs. In a fairy-tale result, the Kings knocked off the defending champions with Gretzky showing the way. It was revenge. But it wasn't sweet.

Gretzky showed exceptional poise, assuming the responsibility that comes with the captain's "C" at a very early age and never faltering.

"I didn't enjoy the series at all," said Gretzky. "It wasn't fun for me. We spent 15 days or whatever it was in the series. I saw those guys every day and we had no words at all. That's not what life is supposed to be all about. You're supposed to be able to talk to your best friends."

The Oilers' demise cleared the path for their arch-rivals from Calgary, and the Flames made the most of it. Helped by some curious coaching decisions from the Kings' Robbie Ftorek, who was fired a few days later, the Flames rolled past L.A. and, after disposing of the Blackhawks, moved to a replay of their first Stanley Cup final.

This time, the Flames were just too strong for the Canadiens. Doug Gilmour had joined Calgary and the Canadiens couldn't keep both him and Mullen under wraps. Between them, they dominated the scoring while Montreal got little from their two top snipers, Bobby Smith and Mats Naslund. Calgary defenseman Al MacInnis was superb, as was goaltender Mike Vernon, and despite a heart-breaking second-overtime loss in Game 3 that put the Flames one game down, they refused to fold and won the next three.

By rights, the Edmonton dynasty should have been dead by this point.

The 1989 final series between Calgary
and Montreal marked the last time
two Canadian teams met in the finals.
This series was also a match-up of two
small market teams who now face
radical restructuring to survive in the
modern NHL market.

Following pages:
Calgary's Theo Fleury clears room in
front of the Calgary net.

Above: Lemieux and Gretzky captured together at Rendez-vous '87 in Quebec City.

Opposite: Gretzky to Lemieux! Mario Lemieux and Wayne Gretzky celebrate after teaming up for one of the most famous goals in Canadian history. During the 1987 Canada Cup final series with the USSR, while using Larry Murphy as a decoy, Gretzky fed a perfect pass to a trailing Lemieux who fired a rising wrist shot past the Soviet goaltender—a rare moment that featured the game's two brightest stars at the height of their powers.

Many of the key players had moved on, but the next year, Sather made a bunch of mid-season trades and rebuilt the team on the fly. He fleeced the Red Wings for four players—Petr Klima, Adam Graves, Joe Murphy and Jeff Sharples—in exchange for Jimmy Carson, Kevin McClelland and a draft pick. Then he traded Sharples for the point man he badly needed, Reijo Ruotsalainen.

For the second year in succession, the Kings knocked off the defending champions in the first round (thereby costing Calgary coach Terry Crisp his job). But Gretzky got hurt, and, when the Kings limped into Edmonton, they were easy pickings for the Oilers. Graves and Murphy joined Gelinas to form a line that had a memorable playoff, and Mark Messier had the best post-season of his career in Edmonton—which says a lot. For the second time in three years, the Oilers breezed past Boston in the finals and, for the fifth time in seven years, they were the Stanley Cup champions.

Had the people who run the game been anywhere near as capable as the people who played it, the '80s would have been a banner decade for the NHL. But that was not the case.

President John Ziegler was under the gun after a series of botch-ups. There was the notorious "Yellow Sunday," Mothers' Day 1988, when NHL officials refused to work a game in New Jersey to protest the action of the Devils' coaching staff. Head coach Jim Schoenfeld had called referee Don Koharski a "fat pig," and assistant coach Doug McKay had bumped him.

Amateur officials wearing yellow sweaters handled the game and Ziegler could not be found to intervene in the dispute.

There was also the Pat Quinn affair. Ziegler had to survive two votes of confidence from the NHL board to get through this one but, because of pending court cases, the governors had little choice.

Once again, the problem started with a contract that had not been registered with the league. In 1986, having been assured on three separate occasions that Quinn, then the coach of the Kings, was free to discuss employment for the following season, Arthur Griffiths, assistant to the chairman of the Vancouver Canucks, delivered an offer.

Right: Dana Murzyn reaches Montreal's Stephane Richer as he uses his body to shield the Calgary defender from the puck.

Below: The Oilers overpowered the Boston Bruins to win the Stanley Cup in 1988. The Cup is the one goal that has, so far, eluded future Hall of Famer and Boston Captain Ray Bourque.

Opposite: Oilers Captain Mark Messier holds the Stanley Cup high after leading his team to victory over the Boston Bruins in the 1990 Stanley Cup Final. This cup was especially important because it showed that Messier was capable of winning without Wayne Gretzky, who was traded to Los Angeles the previous season.

After some negotiation, the two parties agreed to terms. On January 2, 1987, Griffiths delivered a $100,000 signing bonus to Quinn. On January 9, Ziegler made Quinn only the third person in the history of the league to be expelled. He fined the Canucks $310,000 and the Kings $130,000. He said it was, "clear that at some point, everyone forgot … the integrity of the competition."

The Vancouver people were furious. They said that Ziegler's first advice had been to destroy the evidence, that he told them to tear up the contract. When they refused, they said, he fined them. They filed appeals to the board of governors and when those failed, they filed suit. Finally, they won in the British Columbia Supreme Court when it was ruled that Ziegler had acted "in an arbitrary manner … in excess of his jurisdiction." The judge reduced the fine to $10,000 and said that Quinn had done nothing wrong.

Ziegler's close friend Alan Eagleson, head of NHL Players Association, was also running into trouble. Following complaints from players, a dissident group, composed of two player agents—Rich Winter and Ron Salcer—and Ed Garvey, the former head of the union for National Football League players, tried to unseat Eagleson.

When the decade ended, Eagleson was still in place, but he wouldn't stay that way for long.

As far as most fans are concerned, however, the decade belonged to Gretzky and the Oilers. They won five Stanley Cups and, had they stayed together, might have produced the greatest dynasty hockey, and perhaps all sport, has ever known.

"There were a lot of good things about that team that probably won't be repeated," said Sather wistfully.

For the most part, they took good care of themselves and you didn't have to police them. I loved watching their games and the practices were even better. The highlight to me was playing a little game with Wayne. We used to get guys in the middle or play three-on-three. I liked to play against Wayne because you could never get the puck off him. We'd play that after practice and we'd play for another hour lots of times, but it was such fun to watch him do what he could do. It was like a grown guy in the NHL playing with a bunch of four- and five-year-olds, he was so much better than us.

I was pretty young and in pretty good shape and all the other guys were players and we couldn't get the puck off him. He'd do what he wanted and laugh about it. It was a real hoot. I think that was the most enjoyable part.

But we were riding from Philadelphia to New York one time and somebody had brought a list of the top 100 salaries of athletes. Wayne was right at the bottom in salaries but he was the one who dominated his sport the most. I said, "You know what's going to break this team up? Money." And that's what it was.

If you could have kept them together, who knows what you could have done? That year that the team was dismantled, they were all such great players and they were just at that point when they started to peak. Think how many points Wayne would have got if he'd played with those guys for the rest of his career—Glenn Anderson, Mark Messier, Jari Kurri, and all those guys who could do things with the puck. He might have got 90 goals three or four years in a row. That's the sad part about it.

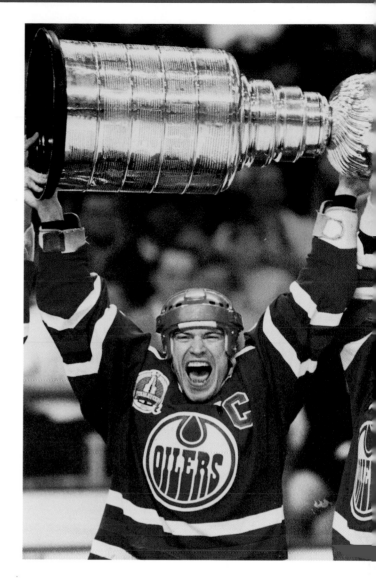

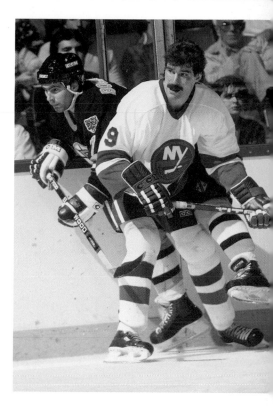

Left: Head over heels: Denis Potvin upends a Minnesota North Star in a 1981 final game.

Above: Clark Gillies provided a valuable physical presence for the talent-rich Islanders.

Below: Bossy's backhand is stopped by a sprawling Pittsburgh goaltender.

Opposite: Tonelli tries to dig the puck out from beneath the Penguins' goalie.

Following pages: The front of the Islanders net was a dangerous place to linger in the 1980s. The New York defense tosses a pair of Penguins forwards to provide their goalie, Billy Smith, a clear view of the puck.

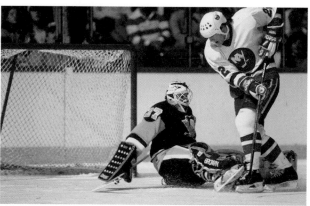

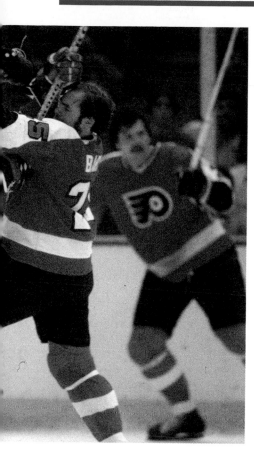

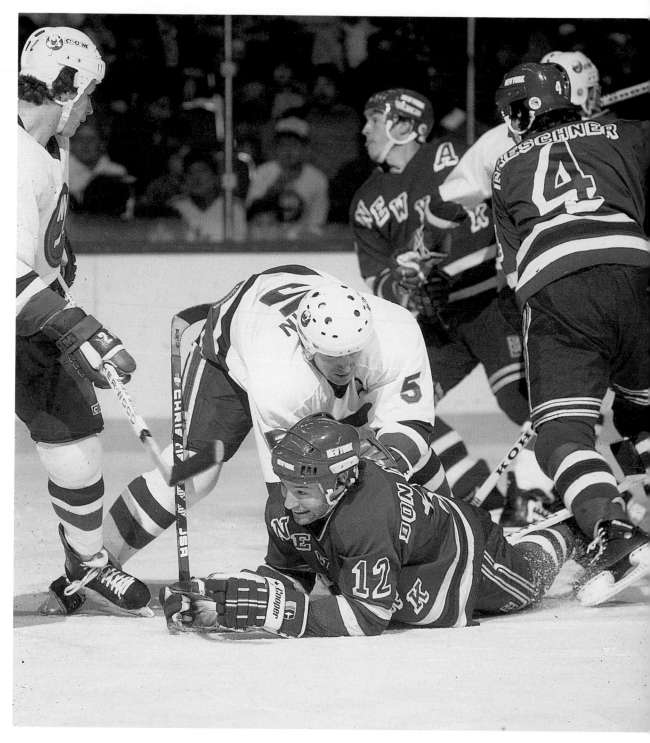

Opposite far left: Although the Islanders of the 1980s were far superior to the Rangers, games between New York's two NHL teams still generated a great deal of excitement.

Above: In their first cup appearance, the Islanders clashed with the Philadelphia Flyers, an older, more experienced version of the "Broad Street Bullies" who had terrorized the NHL in the early 1970s.

Left: Brian Trottier stands up Edmonton's Lindstrom in the tight-checking 1984 final series.

Right: Potvin won the Norris trophy three times during his NHL career and was elected to the Hockey Hall of Fame in 1991.

Left: Using the net to shield off a New Jersey defender, Gretzky circles the goal with his patented wraparound.

Below: Billy Smith defends his crease as he cuts the legs out from under an airborne Wayne Gretzky. The Islanders beat the Oilers in four straight to win the Cup in 1983, with Smith winning the Conn Smythe Trophy.

Right: Oilers' agitator Esa Tikkanen is tied up by the Bruins' Willi Plett.

Following pages:

A linesman works to separate Mark Messier from a Flyers player behind the Philadelphia net.

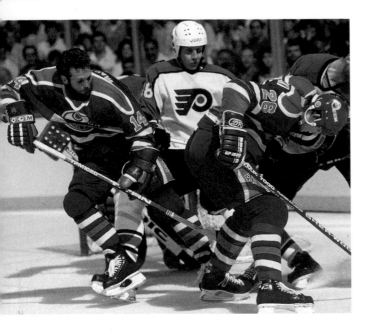

Above: Craig MacTavish (without helmet) looks for a loose puck in the skates of Mike Krushelynksi and Kjell Samuelsson.

Above right: Gretzky's patented wraparound move fooled hundreds of goalies throughout his magnificent career.

Below: The Great One takes flight after a collision with Billy Smith in 1983. This was one of two great final series between the young Oilers and the veteran Islanders.

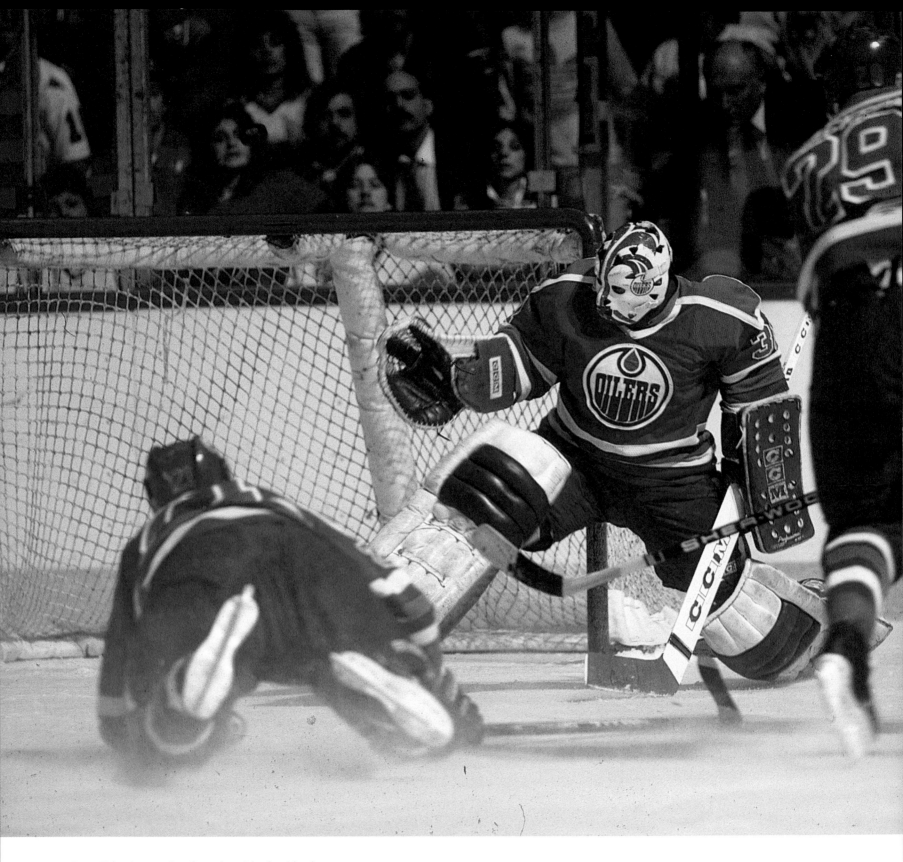

Grant Fuhr gloves a shot from the stick of an Islanders
forward. With Fuhr in nets the Oilers beat the Islanders
to win their first Cup in 1984.

Above: Paul Coffey, one of the NHL's highest scoring defensemen, was an integral part of the Edmonton team that won four Cups in the 1980s. With his soft hands and blazing speed, Coffey was the perfect fit for a young, fast team with a wide-open offense.

Below: Solid defenseman Steve Smith fences with a New Jersey Devils player.

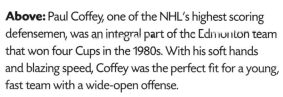

It is the particular genius of Mario Lemieux that the most remarkable achievement of his 12-year career is not immortalized in the National Hockey League record book or engraved on any trophy, but lives on largely in the memories of those who witnessed it in person or viewed it on television.

The day began with a visit to a medical clinic in suburban Beaver County, Pennsylvania for the 20th and final radiation treatment for the nodular lymphocytic form of Hodgkin's disease. Lemieux was diagnosed with the illness soon after Christmas in the 1992–93 season. During a routine check of his cranky back, Lemieux asked doctors an innocent question about a lump that had developed on his neck. A biopsy showed Lemieux had developed cancer in a lymph node.

On the morning of his final radiation treatment, Lemieux left the clinic in search of a commercial flight to Philadelphia. When none was available, he chartered a private plane and arrived at the Spectrum just before the start of his team's game (Mar. 2, 1993) against the Flyers, a bitter rival in the ongoing Battle of Pennsylvania. From a cancer ward to a hockey arena in less than 12 hours and with no physical training allowed during his convalescence, Lemieux scored two points—a goal and an assist—in a 5-4 Penguins' loss. He received accolades from players on both sides, but the most stirring tribute of all came from the

Stopping on a dime, Lemieux tries to roll the puck past the Quebec goaltender.

sellout crowd. Usually notorious Penguins' baiters—and especially tough on Mario—they rewarded him with a standing ovation.

In many ways, Lemieux served as a symbol for the 1990s. His career paralleled many of the developments, both good and bad, of the era in which he was the dominant player.

It was a time when the NHL tiptoed gently into the real world, an era when villains and felons shared the focus with innovators and creators. It was a time when a chariman of the board of governors, Bruce McNall, was jailed for fraud; when a Hall Of Famer and founder of the NHL Players' Association, Alan Eagleson, was imprisoned for racketeering; when a former *Hockey News* Man Of The Year, junior coach Graham James, was jailed for sexual abuse. It was a period when a team's comptroller, not its coach or general manager, was frequently the most influential member of the front office.

Lemieux began the new decade by helping his Penguins win back-to-back Stanley Cups in 1991 and 1992. In doing so, Mario finally fulfilled the promise of his surname, *le mieux:* the best. It was a time when so many of the game' star players fought to overcome serious injury. Lemieux himself endured two major back operations, one of which kept him on the sidelines for the entire 1994–95 season. Lemieux eventually beat cancer, as did his former teammate John Cullen and popular referee Paul Stewart, but Doug Wickenheiser, the first player chosen in the 1980 entry draft, succumbed to the disease, at age 37, midway through the 1998–99 season.

Lemieux was also at the forefront of the explosive salary escalation that occurred in the decade. In 1992, he signed what was a wholly unprecedented contract for hockey— six years, $42 million.

On the ice, Lemieux saw the NHL catering to its lowest common denominator, as constant expansion diluted the player pool. Vocal in his disenchantment

After winning two Stanley Cups as a teammate of Mario Lemieux, Jaromir Jagr has emerged as one of the world's best players since the retirement of his teammate and mentor. The captain of the Pittsburgh Penguins, Jagr is one of a select few players capable of dominating a game whenever they are on the ice. Jagr was also a vital member of the Czech Republic team that won the Gold Medal at the 1998 Winter Olympics.

One of the greatest ever to play the game, Mario Lemieux, with his grace and skill, was a joy to watch and a nightmare to defend. Scoring a goal on his first shift in the NHL and marking a hat trick in his final game, Lemieux had a way of making the big play. He won two Stanley Cups in Pittsburgh and three Hart Trophies. Lemieux was plagued with health problems throughout his 12-year career. Back injuries made it painful for him to even lace up his skates. Lemieux was diagnosed with Hodgkin's disease during the 1992–93 season and missed a month of the season to undergo radiation therapy. Returning to play immediately following his last treatment, Lemieux still managed to lead the league in scoring and was named the most valuable player. Mario resurrected a struggling franchise when he arrived in Pittsburgh and rewarded fans with two Stanley Cups. Now, two years after his retirement, he may once again be called upon to save the franchise. With the team bankrupt, and Lemieux still owed some 30 million dollars in deferred salary, he has become a part-owner of the Penguins.

An airborne Gretzky reaches for the puck as he flies through the crease.

about the state of the game, Lemieux eventually cowed the league into making changes to free up the ice for its skilled players.

He also served as a mentor to the talented Czech Jaromir Jagr—Mario Jr. The season Lemieux missed because of injury, he watched his protégé become the first European-trained player to win an NHL scoring title.

Lemieux, a complex and private man, always demonstrated a single-mindedness of purpose. That characteristic was evident on his draft day in 1984 when he refused to pull on a Penguins' sweater because contract talks were stalled, and it was evident 12 years later when, despite significant public criticism, he steadfastly refused to play for Canada in the 1996 World Cup. The fact that he made only the one international appearance on behalf of Canada doesn't detract from the result of that appearance, however. In the 1987 Canada Cup tournament, Lemieux took a pass from Wayne Gretzky and, with Larry Murphy providing the screen, fired a high wrist shot in the dying moments of play to give Canada the series over Russia—a play for the ages.

Unlike Gretzky, he was not always the most well-spoken ambassador for the game. Like Bobby Orr, you always wondered how magnificent Mario could have been had injuries and illness not coaxed him out of the game at age 31. Some wonder if Lemieux ever truly loved playing the game, but he had to in order to overcome all the obstacles that crossed his path through 12 mostly sensational seasons.

Without question, he was the most watchable player of his generation, blessed with a combination of skill and strength that the game had never seen before—and may not see again. The fact that he retired with 613 goals in only 745 games suggests his greatness may never truly be appreciated.

For Lemieux, the road became an obstacle course in July of 1990 when he had surgery to remove a herniated disk from his back. He spent the better part of six months rehabilitating his injury and recovering from an infection, which forced him to miss the first 50 games of the Penguins' season. Lemieux returned and produced a wholly presentable

45 points in 26 games, but every day, the threat was there—that he'd have to pull himself out of the line-up if his back pain flared up. Once, in the 1991 Stanley Cup finals against the Minnesota North Stars, Lemieux missed a game (the third in the series) because his back went into spasms as he laced up his skates. All through the playoffs, he slept with a plywood board under his hotel mattress to provide extra support. In the end, he scored 44 playoff points to win the Conn Smythe trophy as the playoff MVP and to lift the Penguins to their first-ever championship.

Up until the '90s, the pattern in the NHL was that if you won a Stanley Cup, the odds were enhanced that you would win again. The era of the dynasty would eventually end, but not until the Penguins overcame long odds to repeat as champions the next year. In preparing Team USA for the 1991 Canada Cup, Penguins' coach Bob Johnson suffered a stroke on the eve of the

Sergei Fedorov was the first European to win the Hart Trophy as the NHL's most valuable player in the 1993–94 season. He also won the Selke Trophy as the league's top defensive forward the same year and again in 1995–96.

tournament. Casting around for a possible replacement, Pittsburgh general manager Craig Patrick settled on his director of player development, William (Scott) Bowman. Bowman had joined the Penguins' organization two seasons earlier after having been out of hockey since the Buffalo Sabres dismissed him in December 1986. Bowman maintained his Buffalo residence even as he worked for the Penguins. With the 1991–92 season about to begin, there was much uncertainty about Johnson's prognosis for recovery. Accordingly, Bowman stepped into the breach on an interim basis in the beginning. Bob Johnson died in November, and the Penguins, dedicating their season to the late Johnson, spent the better part of that season sorting themselves out—they were just an

Above: After winning the Stanley Cup in 1997, some of "The Russian Red Wings," Igor Larionov, Slava Kozlov, and Slava Fetisov, took the Stanley Cup to Red Square in Moscow. The trip marked the first time that the Cup traveled to Russia.

Opposite: Known for his intensity and his unorthodox style, Hasek became one of hockey's greatest stars in the 1990s. In 1996–97 he won both the Vezina Trophy as the league's top goaltender and the Hart Trophy as the league's most valuable player. He repeated this feat the following season.

87-point team—before defending their championship in the playoffs. The urge to coach again eventually gripped Bowman and in 1993, after one more season behind the Pittsburgh bench, he joined the Detroit Red Wings as their head coach.

Bowman's career covered four decades, but it was in the 1990s that his place in the history books was firmly etched. Bowman coached his 1,607th regular-season game on December 29, 1995, moving past Al Arbour to become the all-time leader in games coached. Midway through the 1996–97 season, he became the only coach ever to win 1,000 regular-season games. He followed that by coaching Detroit to back-to-back championships in 1997 and 1998, giving him eight Stanley Cups in his coaching career and equalling Toe Blake's career record. Not bad for someone who thought his coaching days were done when he finished up in Buffalo. That year, his children gave him as a gift a vanity license plate that read, "NHL 739," which was how many wins he had registered to that point in his career. He was still driving around with that license plate years later when he won his 1,000th game.

"Nobody, at least in my lifetime, will come close to that," said Larry Robinson, the former Los Angeles Kings' coach. "I don't know how anyone can last that long."

Bowman will be the first to admit that, for much of his career, he won consistently in part because he was blessed with so many talented players. Bowman relied heavily on established NHLers, believing in a simple formula for success—that you win in the NHL with NHLers. Accordingly, Bowman rarely provided on-the-job training to teenagers, fresh out of Junior—and when he did (in Buffalo, for example, with 18-year-olds Phil Housley and Tom Barrasso), the results were generally mixed. In Detroit, Bowman borrowed an idea from the legendary Soviet coach, Viktor Tikhonov, who believed in deploying players as five-man units, giving them an opportunity to learn each other's habits and tendencies.

Bowman occasionally used five Russian players together on the ice and, when the Red Wings won their first Cup, Igor Larionov, Slava Fetisov, and Slava Kozlov celebrated by taking the venerated trophy on

Switching to his backhand Alexander Mogilny slides the puck between the pads (five hole) on a fallen Tommy Salo.

the road to Moscow. In a heady three-day trip, Larionov and Co. put it on display in Red Square, marking the first time the Stanley Cup had gone abroad to Russia.

In all, nine European-born players had their names engraved on the 1998 Stanley Cup, one more than the year before. The Red Wings' back-to-back championships put a punctuation mark on a trend that began in 1973 when the Maple Leafs first signed Sweden's Borje Salming. By 1999, almost a quarter (23.9%) of the players in the NHL were born outside of North America. In 1994, Sergei Fedorov became the first Russian player to win the Hart Trophy as the league's most valuable player. The same year, Dominik Hasek became the first Czech to win the Vezina Trophy as the league's top goalie. For years, teams had limited themselves to a real (but unofficial) quota of import players, on the grounds that you couldn't develop the proper team chemistry with more than half-a-dozen or so European players in the line-up. By 1999, two of the league's most successful teams, the Ottawa Senators and the Pittsburgh Penguins, each had a dozen Europeans on their 24-man rosters. Geographically, borders were changing across Europe, and in the NHL, the more forward-thinking teams reaped the benefit of a what had turned into a full-fledged migration.

The stereotyping of Europeans started to break down for the most practical of reasons. Continued NHL expansion saw the demand for players badly outstrip the supply. The Original 21 had become 28 by October, 1999, and two more teams—the Minnesota Wild and the Columbus Blue Jackets—were set to enter the league in the fall of 2000. With talent spread so thinly, teams were forced to search even harder for players whenever they could find them. Los Angeles Kings general manager, Dave Taylor, put it this way: the NHL needed to develop players, no matter what the source—Red Army or Red Deer, Alberta.

"It's unique that our sport is played by so many countries at a high level," said Pierre Gauthier, the Anaheim Mighty Ducks' general manager. "The best players in the world play in the NHL. That's the strength of our league and that's come to the forefront in the last decade and it's only going to continue to grow."

Apart from their on-ice successes, the Red Wings were also leaders at the box office. In the early part of the decade, Detroit usually ran one-two with the Calgary Flames in terms of overall attendance. For a five-year span, both teams averaged above 19,000 fans per game. The Red Wings were able to maintain their attendance numbers throughout the decade. By contrast, the Flames saw their fortunes—on and off the ice—slip dramatically. Early in the decade, the Flames regularly challenged for the NHL's overall title. By the end, they were touch-and-go to qualify for the playoffs. Their decline mirrored a most discouraging development: the league's shrinking Canadian content. In 1990, the NHL was a 21-team league, with seven franchises based in Canada. In 1999, it was a 28-going-on-30 team league, with only six teams remaining in Canada.

The Quebec Nordiques shifted to Denver for the start of the 1995–96 season. Rechristened the Colorado Avalanche, they won a Stanley Cup in their inaugural season. The next season, the Winnipeg Jets shifted to Phoenix and became the Coyotes. For the first time in NHL history, there were more teams south of the Mason-Dixon line than north of the 49th parallel.

Essentially, the Nordiques and Jets' exodus shared one common trait. They were unable to get the financing, either privately or publicly, for new arenas. The 1990s saw an unprecedented building boom sweep across the league. The seeds for what was a major revolution in professional sport were quietly sewn in the late 1980s when Bill Davidson, the owner of the National Basketball Association's Detroit Pistons, struck upon a

Perennial playoff contenders since their move to Colorado, the Avalanche have relied on the leadership and consistency of captain Joe Sakic to guide them deep into the playoff rounds.

The new Air Canada Centre in Toronto.

heretofore radical idea: installing luxury suites in a building's prime location. Until then, all private boxes were installed high above the ice surface, which meant the worst seats in the house were also the most expensive. In Davidson's Palace of Auburn Hills, the majority of suites were placed just above the first seating bowl. The Palace was wildly successful and, as a result, NBA and NHL teams rushed to copy the concept. As old buildings were retired and new ones took their place, it became apparent that luxury seating revenue could effectively double a team's gate receipts. This, in turn, created huge economic disparities between teams that could construct spanking new buildings and teams trying to do business the old fashioned way—by ticket sales alone.

The Nordiques and Jets unhappily found themselves priced out of the league. The Nordiques left first, sold to Ascent Entertainment on May 25, 1995. For owner Marcel Aubut and his five limited partners, the end came when Quebec premier Jacques Parizeau rebuffed his attempts for provincial financing for a new 19,000-seat arena. "The new realities of the hockey industry, the size of the Quebec City market and the absence of adequate government help have sounded the death knell for the Nordiques," said Aubut. Aubut, who bought the team from Carling O'Keefe Breweries in 1988 for $14.8 million Canadian dollars, sold it for US$75 million seven years later.

"I am sad and shocked," commented long-time Nordiques' Hall of Fame centre Peter Stastny. "It's unbelievable."

Over time, however, the pressures on Canadian teams became all too believable. In the same week the Nordiques were sold, a grassroots movement in Winnipeg spared the Jets franchise—temporarily. About $13 million was raised in a week to keep the Jets in town, monies donated by children cracking open piggybanks to seniors endorsing pension checks. The group, which was eventually incorporated as Spirit Of Manitoba Inc., failed to meet a mid-August deadline for raising $111 million, which would have paid for the team and created an endowment fund to cover the club from further financial losses.

The sale—from Barry Shenkarow to Minneapolis businessman Richard Burke for US$65 million—went through (in August 1996), again because the Jets could not get the financing for a new building. The Jets played their final season in Winnipeg as a lame-duck franchise and exited the league in April 1997 to a noisy, tearful ovation, following their six-game loss to the Detroit Red Wings in the opening playoff round.

Of the six Canadian survivors, four moved into new digs in the 1990s. The Senators vacated the old Ottawa Arena for the Corel Centre; the Canucks moved from the Coliseum to GM Place; the Canadiens transferred from the Montreal Forum to the Molson Centre; and the Leafs moved from Maple Leaf Gardens to Air Canada Centre.

The two Alberta-based teams did extensive renovations to their existing structures in order to bring their buildings up to date. Edmonton's Skyreach Centre (née the Northlands Coliseum) and the Canadian Airlines Saddledome (née the Olympic Saddledome) redid the entire lower seating area to install luxury boxes and private clubs.

Below: At just 5′6″ and 160 pounds, Fleury has proven he can play against far bigger players. Shown here, Fleury jousts for the puck with Eric Lindros, one of the most physically imposing players in the NHL.

Original Six Rinks

Top: Maple Leaf Gardens

Above: Chicago Stadium

Left: The Montreal Forum

Above: Madison Square Garden

Far left: The Detroit Olympia

Left: Boston Garden

Eric Lindros

The rush to modern surroundings also cost the NHL a piece of its history, as some of the NHL's most historic buildings disappeared. Apart from the Forum and Maple Leaf Gardens, the league also lost two other shrines from the Original Six—the Chicago Stadium and the Boston Garden. Once Maple Leaf Gardens closed, the oldest building in the league was the Igloo in Pittsburgh. In all, 20 of 28 teams now operate in buildings less than 10 years old, effectively negating any economic advantage that luxury seating (the decade's new buzzword) provided in the first place.

For the remaining Canadian teams, three factors—comparatively high taxes, rising salaries and a falling dollar—made it difficult for all but the Maple Leafs to compete with their U.S. counterparts. The Maple Leafs' television revenues provide them with a financial cushion that the remaining five teams do not enjoy. In November, 1991, the Canadian dollar peaked at 89.3 cents U.S. By August of 1998, it had fallen to 64 cents. Effectively, that meant that a team operating with a $50 million budget saw its spending power decline by more than 25 percent. The bulk of its costs (salaries, travel) were paid out in U.S. dollars. The majority of its revenues (gate receipts, TV, merchandise) came in in Canadian dollars.

A par dollar, according to the NHL's chairman of the board, Harley Hotchkiss, would solve many of the challenges facing Canada's teams heading into the next decade.

Beyond the weak Canadian dollar, there was the matter of rising salary costs. The average NHL player earned $271,000 a year in 1990. By 1999, the average salary had risen to $1.3 million U.S. In 1990, there were fewer than 20 millionaire players and only two—Wayne Gretzky and Mario Lemieux—earned above $2 million per season. By 1999, there were 75 players earning above $2.5 million per season.

The astonishing rise in player salaries can largely be traced to a handful of contracts, one of which resulted from Eric Lindros's most curious entry to the NHL. The Quebec Nordiques chose Lindros, the most highly regarded entry-level player since Mario Lemieux, first overall in the 1991 entry draft. However, Lindros balked at joining the Nordiques, a team that was in the midst of a rebuilding process that would see it miss the playoffs for five consecutive years. No matter what the Nordiques did, Lindros was positively resolute—he would not sign with them. By June of 1992, the Nordiques had determined that Lindros would not waver from his position and held a much publicized auction for his rights.

The bids for the services of an unproven 19-year-old were so attractive that owner Marcel Aubut essentially traded him twice—first to the Philadephia Flyers, then to the New York Rangers. It was high comedy for all but the principals involved in the transaction. Both the Rangers and Flyers argued that they had entered into a binding agreement with the Nordiques. In the end, the NHL was obliged to turn the matter over to an independent arbitrator, Larry Bertuzzi, to resolve this messy, public-relations blunder. Bertuzzi ultimately ruled in favor of the Flyers' staggering offer of players and draft choices: Peter Forsberg, Steve Duchesne, Kerry Huffman, Mike Ricci, Chris Simon, Ron Hextall, plus two No. 1 picks. It went into the record books as one of the biggest trades in league history. After surrendering almost a third of their team to get one player, the Flyers were also obliged to step up with what was then an unprecedented contract for a first-year player—$3.5 million per season for the next five years.

Two years later, in the spring of 1993, the Senators agreed to a similar mind-boggling financial package for their No. 1 draft choice, Alexandre Daigle. If NHL general managers could understand the fuss over Lindros— as a junior-aged player, he played for Canada in the 1991 Canada Cup— they couldn't comprehend why Ottawa would lavish so generous a deal on the unproven Daigle, $12 million for five years. No one projected Daigle as the second coming of Mario Lemieux, even though he was being paid that way. Daigle's contract set a new standard for entry-level players that lasted only one more year before the league said, "Enough."

In an era when only the most precocious of talents made an impact in their first three seasons, the league found itself paying small fortunes to 18-year-olds for their potential, not their results. Of all the concessions wrung from the players in the 103-day lockout of 1994–95 season, the most significant was the salary cap for entry-level players.

Ron Hextall does the splits as a pair of Canadiens try to stuff the puck by him.

Disgraced hockey czar Alan Eagleson

On the whole, labor unrest in the NHL followed sweeping changes at the top of both the NHL and the NHL Players' Association heirarchy. Alan Eagleson's iron-fisted control of the Players Association had begun to dwindle in the late '80s as an alliance of player agents and former NHLers questioned his handling of their affairs. Eventually, the evidence against Eagleson's handling of the NHLPA's finances was so overwhelming that he agreed to step aside—and was eventually disbarred, disgraced, and jailed. A search committee headed by the Hartford Whalers' Kevin Dineen pored over a list of potential candidates and settled on a relatively obscure player agent named Bob Goodenow to replace Eagleson. Goodenow was introduced as the deputy director of the NHLPA during the 1990 all-star festivities in Pittsburgh. Publicly, the NHLPA envisioned a year-long phase-in program, but Goodenow essentially took control of the organization as soon as he arrived on the scene. For much of his reign, Goodenow positioned himself as the anti-Eagleson. From a players' perspective, Eagleson's relationship with former NHL president John Ziegler was simply too cozy. Goodenow immediately distanced himself from Ziegler by engineering a 10-day player strike in the spring of 1992 that threatened to cancel the 1991–92 playoffs. The two sides came to what was clearly a stop-gap agreement designed to get the playoffs in. It was obvious, however, that player unrest would eventually coalesce into something more serious.

Soon after the strike was settled, NHL owners removed Ziegler from office. He was replaced on an interim basis by Gil Stein for a five-month period until early 1993. Ziegler was characterized as a do-nothing president in many quarters, but he had one prophetic observation on the day he stepped down—that the league's changing economics would be an issue that just wouldn't go away.

Ziegler asked:

Will the players' share of the revenues become so burdensome that you are pretty much doomed to losing substantial monies if you don't finish in the conference championships? If you operate this business so that the only way you make money is to win, you guarantee losers in your business every year. Beause one thing I can predict every year is, we'll have a first-place team and a last-place team. And if by finishing in last place, you automatically lose money, then I don't think you're running your business very well.

It wasn't the first time the issue of hockey as a business would come up in the ensuing months. In the wake of Ziegler's departure, the office of president was abolished. A search committee to find his replacement eventually settled on Gary Bettman, who was hired to become the league's first commissioner. Bettman joined the NHL from the National Basketball Association where, among other achievements, he was considered the architect of that organization's pioneering salary cap. Bettman possessed a broad base of knowledge in certain areas—television, marketing, labor relations—but lacked an insider's perspective on the game itself.

On the day he took over, his priority was to establish labor peace with the players through a new collective bargaining agreement. The skirmishes with the players' association began almost immediately and by September of 1994, when the gap between the two sides looked chasm-like, the NHL locked out its players. It took almost three-and-a-half months of negotiations before the two sides settled their differences, and that agreement was reached just days before Bettman's deadline for cancelling the season.

In the beginning, there was some question as to which side had won—players or owners—but as time passed, the answer became clear. The player salary spiral that the new CBA was supposed to stem continued unabated. Goodenow stood firm on one issue: no salary cap beyond that for entry-level players. And ownership, given the right to spend as much money on players as they wanted to, did just that.

Once salaries for a handful of star players became entrenched in the system, the arbitration process—or the threat of arbitration—drove up the rest. Cleverly, Goodenow managed to convince the league to twice extend the CBA so that it is now in place until the September 2004 season. The pretext for the second extension was to keep labor peace through the expansion process.

The first was to accomodate the league's plans to participate in the 1998 Winter Olympics in Nagano, Japan. Because of his basketball background, Bettman saw the marketing strides made internationally by the

Eric Lindros had his superstar status confirmed when he was made captain of the Canadian Olympic team, which was made up of the nation's biggest stars.

NBA's participation in the Summer Olympics. Logistically, putting the NHL into the Winter Olympics posed many more significant problems. Summer is basketball's off-season. By contrast, the 15-day window needed for NHL participation falls in February, one of the NHL's busiest and most profitable months. The league weighed the risk of shutting down for three weeks against the reward of international exposure and forged ahead with the plan.

Only two years previously, the NHL had altered the Canada Cup format slightly and rechristened the new tournament the World Cup. From a marketing perspective, the results could not have been better. The USA advanced to the finals against Canada and won the tournament in three games. Ideally, the NHL envisioned a similar result in Nagano and collectively crossed its fingers that a USA victory in men's hockey would provide the same sort of boost to the game's popularity that the 1980 Miracle On Ice in Lake Placid provided.

Publicly, the NHL said all the right things—that its Olympic overture differed substantially from basketball's because, by freeing up players from every country, the NHL could boast up to six Dream Teams, not just one. Privately, the expectation was that one of Canada or the USA, if not both, would play for the gold medal. It didn't happen, of course. With Dominik Hasek providing exceptional goaltending, the Czech Republic won the gold-medal game, edging a Russian team led by the mercurial Pavel Bure. Canada, eliminated in the semifinals in a controversial shootout loss, came up flat in the bronze-medal game against Finland and came home empty-handed. Instead of scoring a public relations coup, the USA, eliminated one round earlier by the Czechs, left with a black eye when members of its men's team trashed a room in the Athlete's Village and then didn't own up to their misdeeds.

Indeed, it was left to the USA women's hockey team to salvage America's developing reputation as a worldwide power. For the first time in history, women's hockey was part of the Olympics. The tournament featured six entries only and one—Japan—qualified as the host country. Only the USA and Canada boasted full-time national women's teams. As a result, they played each other 14 times leading up to

Top: Manon Rheaume.

Bottom: Doug Gilmour tries to slide in a backhand as he flies through the air behind the opposition's net.

the gold-medal game—and it was clear that little separated the two teams. Eight of the 14 games were decided by a goal and three others by two goals. In the end, the USA won the two games that mattered most: a 7–4 win over Canada in the preliminary round and a 3–1 win in the gold-medal game.

Playing goal for Canada in the deciding game was Manon Rheaume, the most visible symbol of the strides made by women's hockey. In the fall of '92, Rheaume received a tryout from the Tampa Bay Lightning and on September 23, made history by becoming the first woman to play an NHL game. Rheaume faced nine shots and stopped seven in an exhibition game against the St. Louis Blues. Later that year, she became the first women to play a professional regular-season game when she played for the Atlanta Knights of the International Hockey League. Shameless publicity stunt or not, Rheaume's appearance for the Lightning brought the first wide-spread attention to the vast strides made by women's hockey.

Canada won the first four women's world hockey championships, so a victory in the Olympics marked a breakthrough for the U.S. women, who were captained by Cammi Granato and ably coached by Ben Smith.

The American women were not the only ones to end a long losing spell in the decade. Apart from the Red Wings, who ended a 42-year drought by winning the Stanley Cup in '97, the Rangers ended a spectacular

Brendan Shanahan is one of the league's premier power forwards. His combination of strength and natural goal-scoring ability made him an integral part of the Red Wings' two Cup victories.

54 years without a championship by winning the 1994 Stanley Cup. Only once in the previous 23 years did the Stanley Cup final go to seven games (in 1987) and many of the principals were back for the reprise. Five members of the '87 Oilers played for the Rangers, including team captain Mark Messier. Mike Keenan, the Rangers' coach, was with the '87 finalists from Philadephia, as was Murray Craven, who played for the

Above: Known as one of the most acrobatic goaltenders in the league, Mike Richter won the Stanley Cup with the Rangers in 1993–94. He was also in nets for Team USA when they won the World Cup in 1996 and again in their less successful Olympic bid in 1998.

Left: The rinkside glass shatters as the Islanders' Bryan Smolinski is pounded into the boards by Boston's Kyle McLaren.

vanquished Vancouver Canucks. Until Messier arrived on the scene, the Rangers were said to be cursed. The details of the curse were vague, however. Legend had it that John Kilpatrick, the Rangers' owner in 1940, was responsible for burning the mortgage papers on Madison Square Garden in the Stanley Cup. For years, the Rangers' players had to listen as the mocking jeer "1940, 1940" followed every unsuccessful bid, which prompted Messier to acknowledge: "We knew if we tried to take on the 54-year history of the Rangers, it would be too much for any team. When you put on a Ranger sweater, you buy into the fact that you are getting inolved in a lot of the history that went down here."

History was of little concern to the Florida Panthers two years later when they advanced to the Stanley Cup final in their only third year of operation. It was the Year of the Rat in south Florida, thanks to a timely extermination by forward Scott Mellanby in the home opener of the 1995–96 season. That night, Mellanby scored two goals in a Panthers'

Above: Devils goalie Martin Brodeur reaches high to make a glove save.

Top right: Brian Leetch spins to evade Philadelphia's John LeClair. Known for his fluid skating style and offensive abilities, Leetch led all playoff scorers and won the Conn Smythe trophy when the Rangers won the Stanley Cup in 1993–94.

Bottom right: The Montreal bench looks on as Gretzky takes flight. Despite reaching the finals with Los Angeles in 1993, No. 99 would never win another Cup after his trade from the Oilers.

win over Calgary. Minutes before game time, he also cornered a rat in the Panthers' dressing room and dispatched it with a hard wrist shot into the wall. The Panthers' goaltender, John Vanbiesbrouck, dubbed this unique achievement a "rat trick" and soon, spectators at aging Miami Arena began to salute their heroes by tossing plastic rats onto the ice. By the time the Panthers advanced to the final against Colorado, it was more than just a passing craze. The ice would get so littered by debris following a Panthers' goal that it would result in lengthy delays. Eventually, the league enacted a rule that would penalize the home team if the deluge of rats continued.

The Panthers were not, however, the first Sunbelt team to flirt with that championship feeling. Gretzky, playing his fifth of eight seasons with the Kings, led them to the 1993 Stanley Cup finals, which they lost to the Montreal Canadiens in five games. It was the pinnacle of Gretzky's time in Los Angeles, a period when going to hockey games in California became oh-so chi chi. The celebrities here once found courtside only at L.A. Lakers' games now pressed their faces up to the glass to watch the Kings. Even the former American president, Ronald Reagan, became a fan and was a frequent visitor in their stirring 1993 run.

That the Canadiens won their 24th Stanley Cup was memorable on a number of different levels, not the least of which was that the momentum in the final series against Los Angeles swung because of an illegal stick. It belonged to Kings' defenseman Marty McSorley and, when the Canadiens called him on it, Los Angeles was ahead 1–0 in the series and 2–1 in the second game. Had the Kings gone up by two games, with the series returning to Los Angeles, the Canadiens would have been hardpressed to rally. As it was, with McSorley in the penalty box and Patrick Roy on the bench for a sixth skater, Montreal tied the game and won in overtime. Eventually, the

Opposite: Patrick Roy blocks off the bottom part of the net as his defenseman rushes to his aid.

Right: Wayne Gretzky leans into a slapshot from the top of the face off circle.

Theoren Fleury, one of the smallest players in the NHL, has overcome his lack of size with his incredible intensity and love for the game. The longtime Calgary Flame uses his speed and shot to make him one of the game's most consistent goal scorers.

Canadiens would win 10 overtime games in a row in the '93 playoffs and Roy took home the Conn Smythe Trophy, in part because of 90-plus shutout minutes in sudden-death overtime. For Gretzky, the disappointment of not winning another Stanley Cup after his departure from Edmonton was keen.

"To come so far and work so hard is a lot harder to accept than losing in the first round or not making the playoffs," Gretzky said, afterwards.

In the end, Gretzky had to settle for establishing what will surely be unassailable marks in the NHL record book. After moving into first place in the all-time points scoring list in 1989, Gretzky added the NHL goals-scoring record (802) to his list of achievements in 1994.

By the end of the 1999 season, he was approaching 2,900 career points, which moved him more than 1,000 points ahead of the runner-up, Gordie Howe, who score 1,850 points. To put it another way, someone would need to score 140 points per season for 20 years to approach Gretzky's career numbers—and even then, he would still not catch him. In a year when a collector had paid $3 million for the ball in which Mark McGwire hit his 70th home run, Swedish-born Tommy Albelin asked: "What will Gretzky's final goal puck be worth? Because his records will never be broken. Never."

Part of the reason was the NHL's new—and in some quarters, unwarranted—fascination with defense. Scoring topped out by the mid-1980s, after which it went into steady decline. The new generation of goaltenders—Hasek, Patrick Roy, Martin Brodeur—led their own assault on the NHL record book. The lack of goalscoring became so contentious an issue that the league eventually sought new ways of limiting the goaltenders' effectiveness and (in theory anyway) putting more offense back into the game.

Innovations in their equipment—making it bigger, but lighter—saw a change in the way goaltenders approached their craft. Equipment started out simply to protect the goaltender. In time, it was designed to help protect the net. As a result, the league introduced limits to the size of equipment, reduced the size of goalcreases, and in general, tried to put a little more sizzle back into the game.

Much of its strategy hinged on the next generation of stars that came on the scene to supplant Lemieux and Gretzky. After Lemieux retired and Gretzky's dominance began to wane, a new generation of multi-nationals rushed in to supplant them among the NHL's elite. Nowadays, the Top 20 is annually sprinkled with players of half a dozen nationalities: not just Canadians and Americans, but Swedes, Finns, Russians, Czechs, Slovaks. The torch was passed—to Jagr and Forsberg, to Paul Kariya and Alexei Yashin, to Teemu Selanne and Ziggy Palffy.

"These young players," said Taylor, "will have to lead the NHL into the next millennium."

And one old player, Lemieux, brought the decade full circle when he emerged in the summer of 1999 as part of a Pittsburgh-based consortium that bought the bankrupt Penguins. The symbolism is just too delicious. From player to owner in one decade? Now that's progress.

One of Pavel Bure's first games as a Florida Panther was played against the Toronto Maple Leafs. Bure picked up from his holdout where he left off, scoring goals at an unrivaled pace. Unfortunately his return in 1999 was short-lived, as recurring knee problems forced him to sit out the end of the regular season, with the Panthers failing to reach the playoffs.

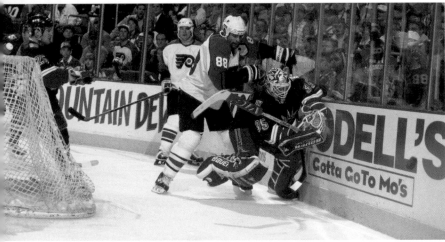

Top: A timely hit from Lindros often swings the momentum of a game.

Bottom: Mike Richter dives out of the way as big Lindros bears down on him.

Right: At over 6'4" and 240 pounds, Lindros often overpowers opposing defenders on his way to the net. His great strength and famous mean streak make him one of the most intimidating players in the game. Lindros won the Hart Trophy in 1994–95 and led the Flyers to the Stanley Cup Finals in 1997 where they lost to the Detroit Red Wings. Despite all of Lindros' accomplishments he still comes under fire from critics who feel that, with all his talent, he should have brought the Stanley Cup to Philadelphia. Lindros is no stranger to controversy. In 1991 the Nordiques drafted him first overall but he refused to report. He elected to play an extra year of junior hockey rather than report to Quebec. The Nordiques eventually capitulated and sent Lindros to Philadelphia in a blockbuster trade that provided the Nordiques with the pieces they needed to win the Stanley Cup, after their move to Colorado and subsequent name change.

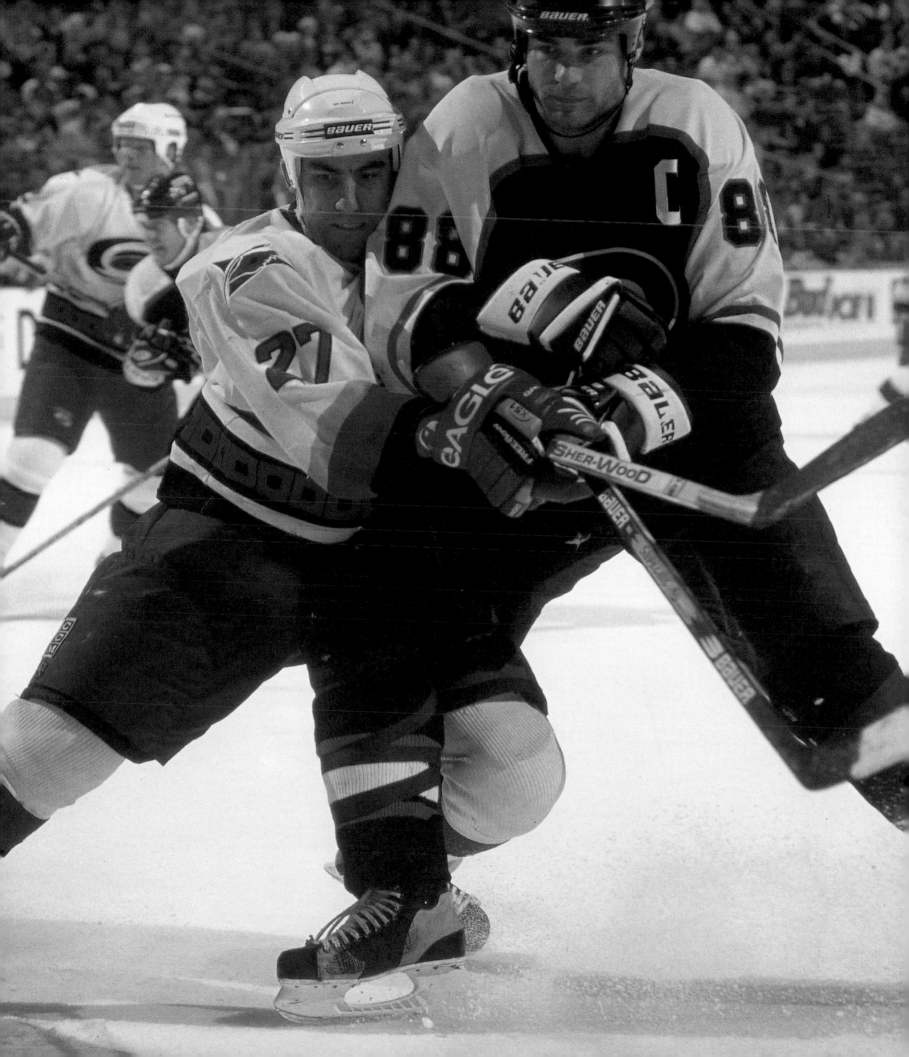

Forsberg holds off an Islander checker with one arm as he chases after a loose puck.

Right: Forsberg keeps his eyes on the play as a Buffalo defenseman rides him into the boards during a game at the Marine Midland Arena in Buffalo.

Below: Equally dangerous with either a pass or a shot, Peter Forsberg has emerged as one of the best all-around players in hockey.

Opposite: Forsberg cuts across the ice in a cloud of snow.

Left: Forsberg flies across the blueline as his teammates look on from the Colorado bench.

Above: A native of Sweden, Forsberg has excelled on the international stage as well as in North America, playing for Sweden in the World Junior Championship. At the 1996 World Cup and the 1998 Winter Olympics in Nagano, Forsberg played for his father, who coached the Swedish entries.

Left: A large goalie, Roy uses his size to eliminate most scoring options and relies on his reflexes, his glove, and his blocker to stop the rest.

Below: Forsberg was part of the famous trade between Quebec and Philadelphia that sent Eric Lindros to the Flyers. Since going to the Nordiques, Forsberg has become a superstar in his own right, which often leads to the question: Who benefited more from the Lindros trade, the Flyers or the Nordiques/Avalanche?

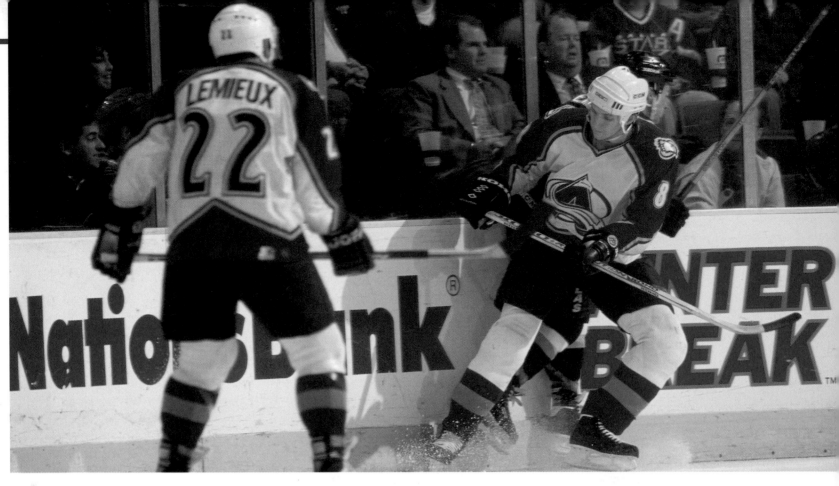

Above: Claude Lemieux watches as teammate Sandis Ozolinsh take his man along the boards. Reviled through much of the NHL for his sometimes dirty play, Lemieux is nonetheless among the league's premier playoff performers and was a major factor in the Avalanche's Cup win.

Right: Sakic won the Conn Smythe trophy in the 1995–96 season as Colorado's NHL team rewarded them with a Stanley Cup victory in their first year of existence. (Formerly the Quebec Nordiques, the team was moved to Colorado before the season began owing to the financial shortcomings of the small-market Nordiques.) Colorado hockey fans found themselves in the enviable position of having a championship-caliber team presented to them intact.

Opposite top left: Forsberg uses his body to protect the puck as a Rangers defenseman tries to manhandle him behind the net.

Opposite top right: A former All-Star, talented Colorado defenseman Sandis Ozolinsh often seems like more of a forward as he creeps into the offensive zone looking for scoring opportunities.

Opposite bottom: It is extremely difficult for the opposition to push Peter Forsberg, known for his superior leg strength and puck control, off the puck.

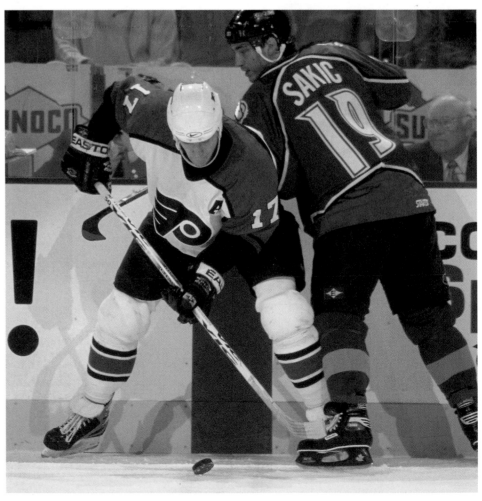

Above: Jaromir Jagr's incredible stamina allows him to play double shifts in almost every game. This great endurance allows the Pittsburgh coaching staff the luxury of having their best player on the ice with two separate lines.

Right: Jaromir Jagr's combination of great reach and strength allow him to keep control of the puck in many difficult situations. In 1998–99 Jagr won the NHL scoring race by over 20 points and won the Hart Trophy. Jagr had an excellent playoffs despite an injured groin and took his team to the second round where they lost to the Toronto Maple Leafs in overtime of the sixth game.

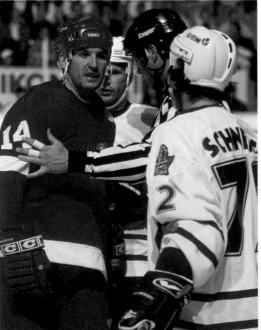

Above: Fedorov rejoined the Red Wings in 1998 after a prolonged hold-out and helped the team to their second Stanley Cup in as many years.

Left: Shanahan is restrained by a linesman during this exchange with Mathieu Schneider of the Maple Leafs.

Left: Adam Graves of the Rangers locks up with Yzerman in the face-off circle.

Above: One of the most respected players in the league, Yzerman has been one of its most consistent offensive performers, scoring over 50 goals five times in his career.

Following pages:
Paul Coffey and Trent Klatt hold their ground as Shanahan enters the Flyers' zone.

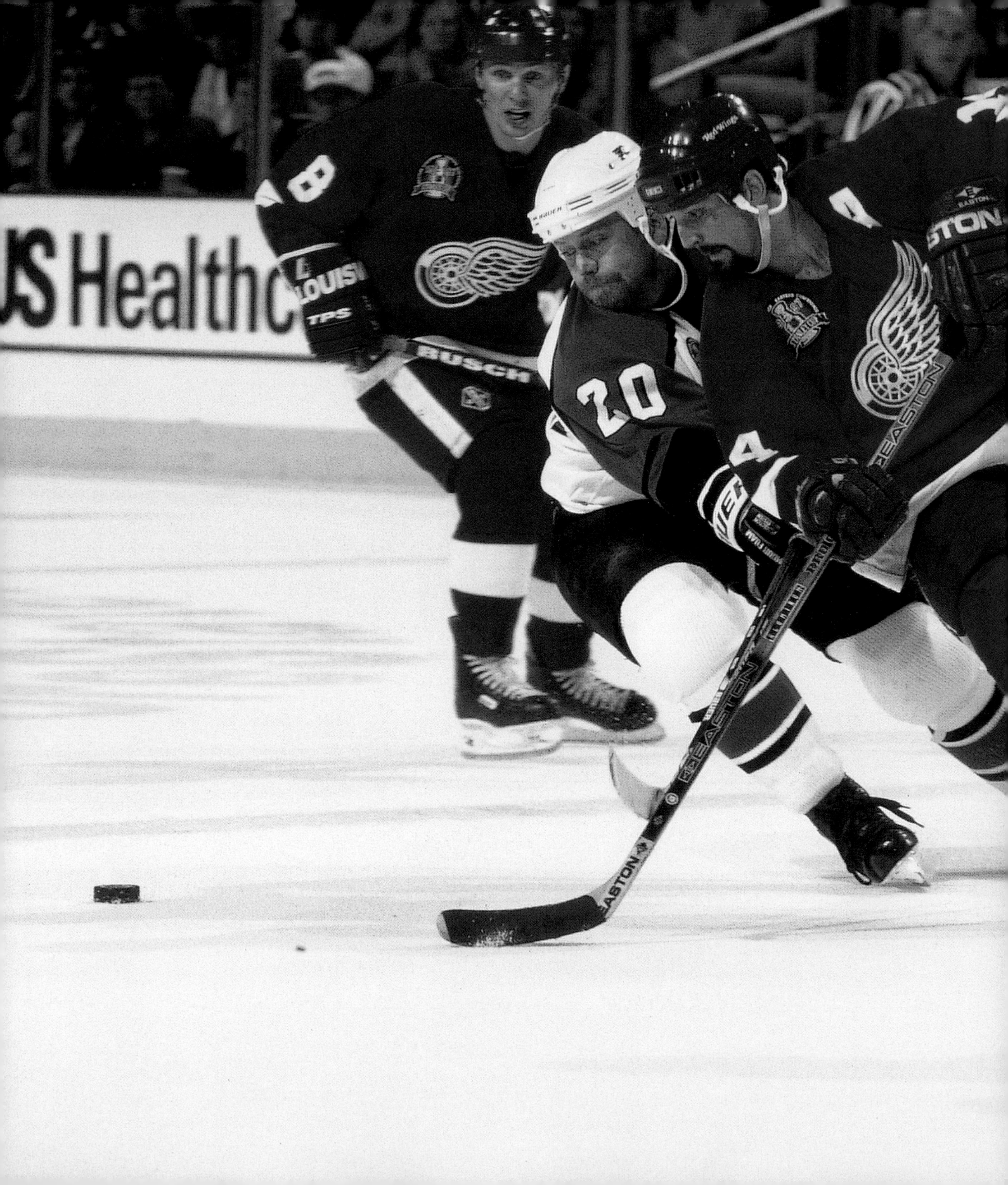

Healthc
TPS
BUSCH
20
EASTON

Always dangerous in front of the net, Brendan Shanahan attracts a crowd of Anaheim defenders.

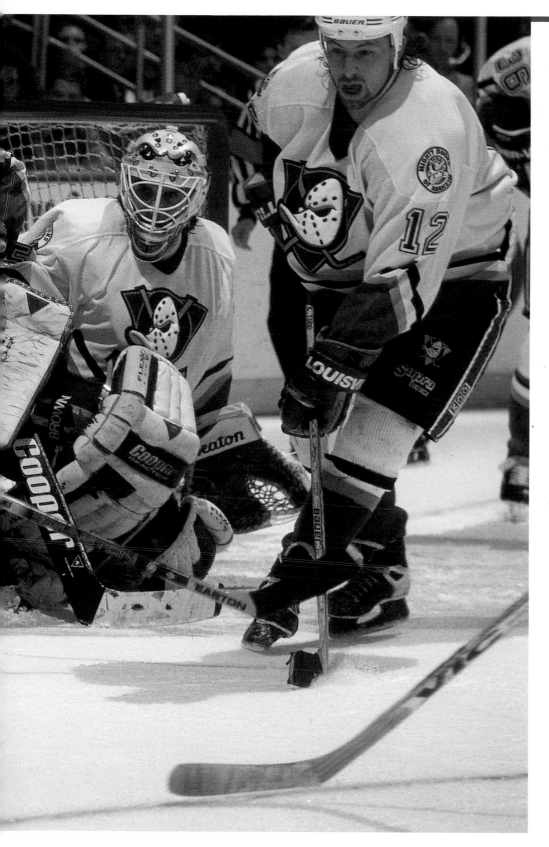

Top: Steve Yzerman takes the puck away from Philadelphia defenseman Petr Svoboda.

Bottom: Steve Yzerman, the longtime Red Wings captain, has scored over 1000 points and won two Stanley Cups over the course of his illustrious career.

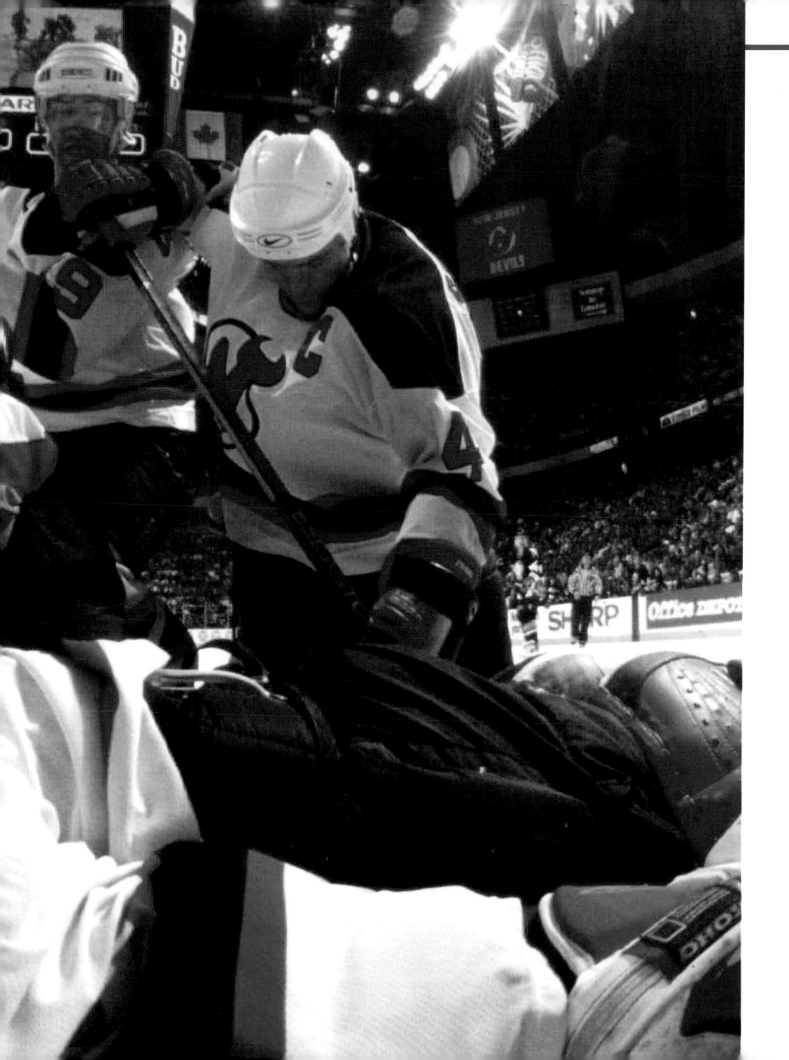

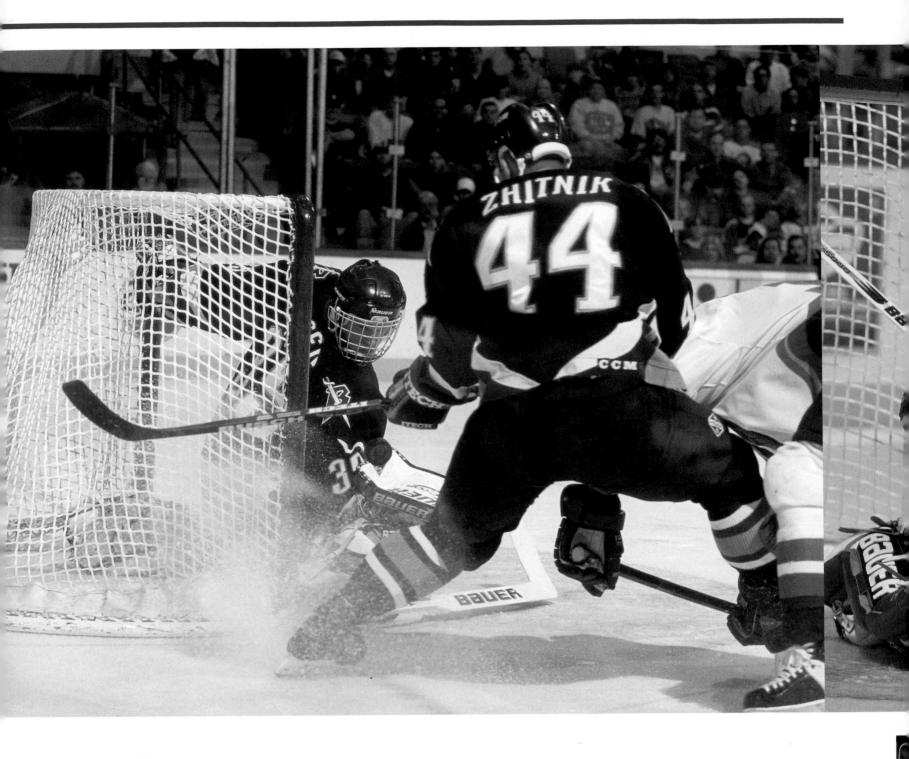

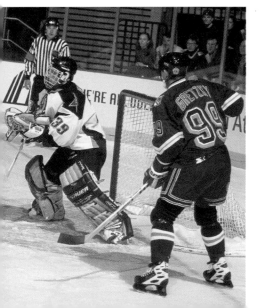

Above: Hasek gets his pads down as a puck floats in on net.

Left: Wayne Gretzky watches from beside the net as a high shot races towards Buffalo goaltender Dominik Hasek's glove hand.

Above right: Hasek gathers himself as he takes a hard shot to the chest.

Above: Mike Modano unleashes a slapshot against the Islanders. In the team's first season in Dallas Modano scored 50 goals.

Right: Dallas teammate Brett Hull has said that Modano is the best player that he has ever played with. Playing together in the NHL for the first time, the pair worked together to win the Stanley Cup in 1998–99.

Left: While playing St. Louis, Brett Hull put together an impressive resume. He won the Hart Trophy in 1990–91, led the NHL in goal scoring for three straight years, scored the tying goal at the 1996 World Cup, and became the St. Louis Blues all-time leading scorer with 527 goals.

Below: As a member of the Stars, Hull played a major role in eliminating his former teammates, the St. Louis Blues, in the second round of the 1998–99 playoffs. Hull picked up an assist on the series' winning goal, scored by teammate Mike Modano.

Opposite top: Always a threat to score, Modano is watched closely by a Calgary player as he looks for open ice to work with.

Following pages:
Hasek has come by his nickname, "The Dominator," honestly. His heroics make his teams instant contenders. This is true of his Buffalo Sabres teams in the 1990s and of the underdog Czech Republic team, which he led to the Gold Medal at the 1998 Winter Olympics.

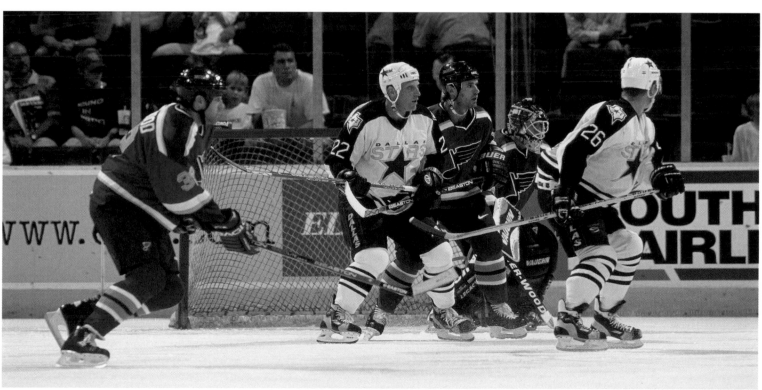

Above: Grant Fuhr extends to make a save. Fuhr was a member of the Maple Leafs in the early 1990s.

Right: Former Maple Leafs Captain Wendel Clark was a fan favorite during his time in Toronto. A dangerous goal scorer and an intimidating physical presence, Clark was traded to the Nordiques as part of the deal that sent present captain Mats Sundin to Toronto.

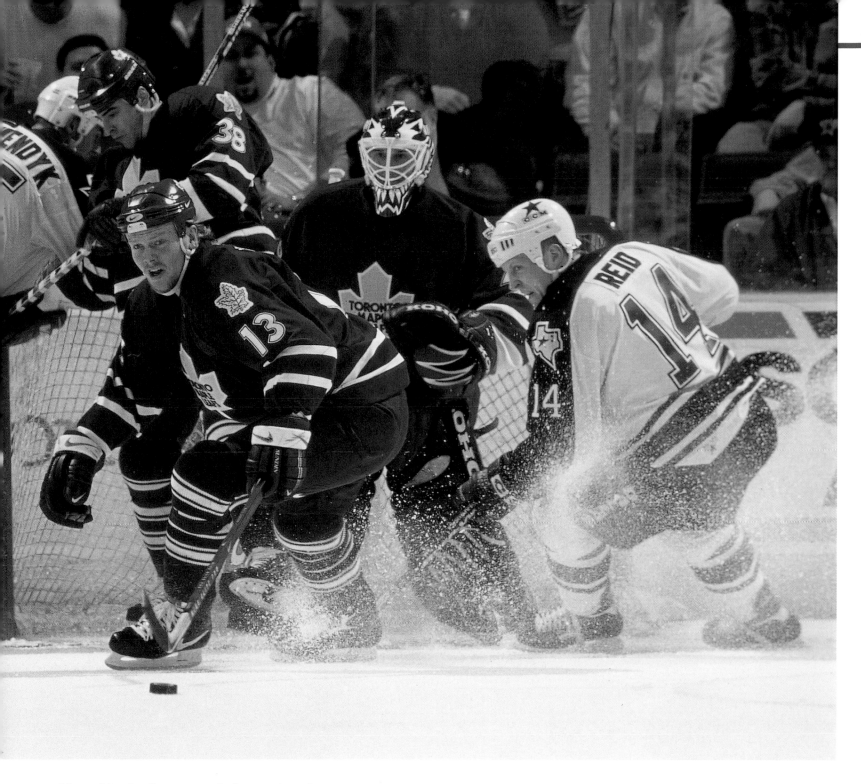

Above: Mats Sundin carves a trail of snow as he gathers the puck in front of the Toronto net.

Opposite: Leafs Assistant Captain Steve Thomas celebrates after scoring the tying goal in a 1999 playoff game with the Philadelphia Flyers. The Leafs would go on to beat the Flyers in six games en route to the conference finals.

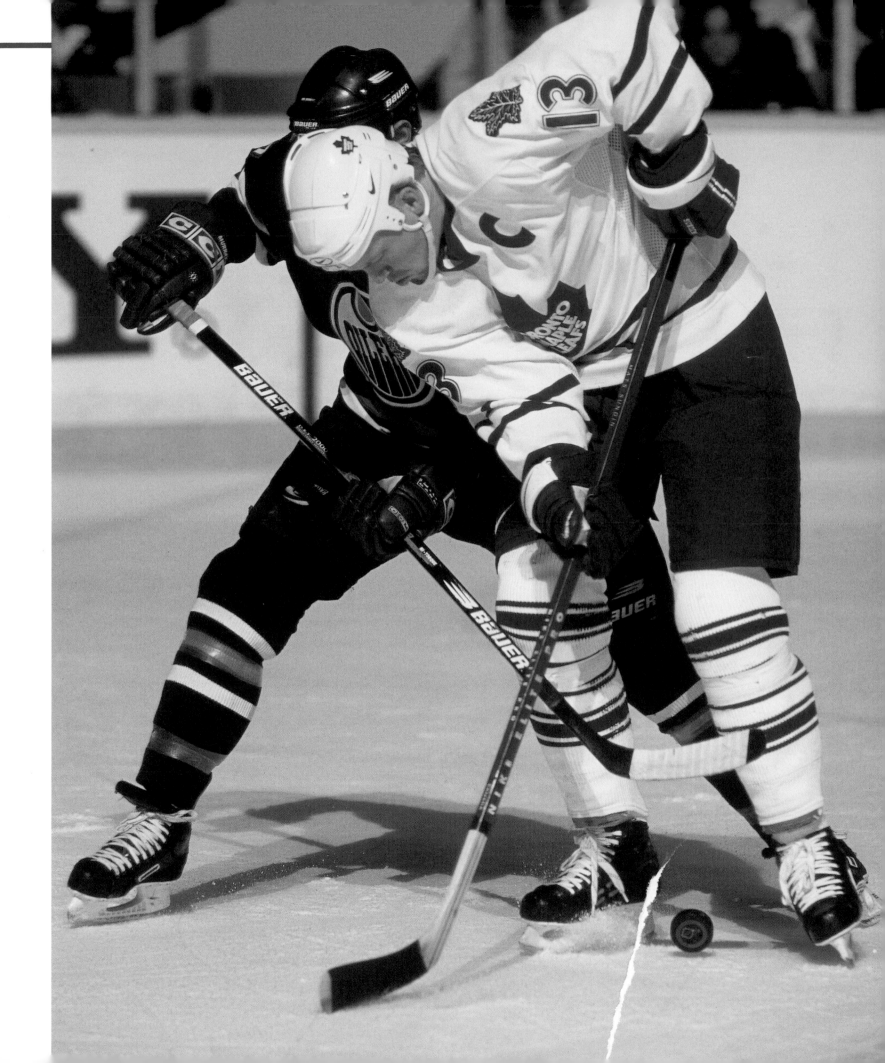

Left: The first European captain of the Maple Leafs, Sundin has always dealt well with the pressure of playing in Toronto. Originally drafted first overall by the Quebec Nordiques in 1989, Sundin was dealt to Toronto in the deal that sent former Leafs captain Wendel Clark to Quebec.

Below: After a disappointing season in 1997–98, Sundin led the Leafs to the Eastern Conference finals in his second year as captain.

Always a dangerous passer, Sundin finds teammate Igor Korolev open as a New Jersey defender closes in.

Opposite: All eyes are on the linesman as a pair of Toronto Maple Leaf captains wait for the puck to drop in a game against their Original Six rivals, the Chicago Blackhawks.

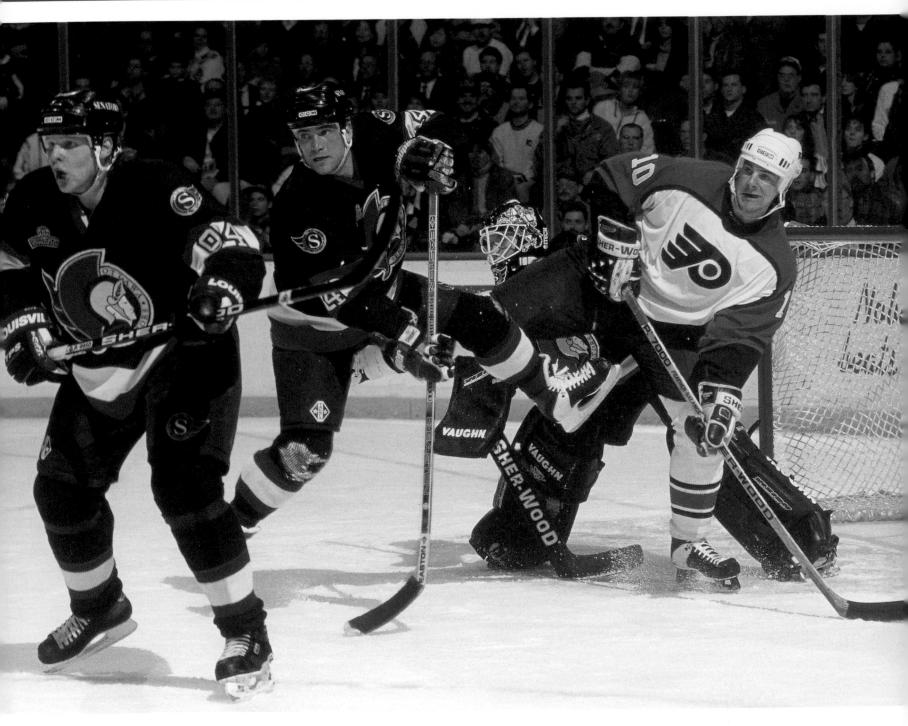

Above: Almost impossible to move when he sets up in front of the opposing goalie, LeClair provides screens for his teammates to fire clean shots for passes that he can deflect into the net.

Opposite top: Sergei Gonchar of the Washington Capitals continues to hook LeClair even as he stoops to recover his stick. Always a threat to score, opponents have learned never to leave LeClair unattended.

Opposite bottom: John LeClair is harried by a pair of St. Louis Blues defensemen. In 1994–95, when he played on the Legion of Doom line with Eric Lindros and Mikael Renberg, the trio physically dominated opponents and each finished the year in the top 10 in scoring.

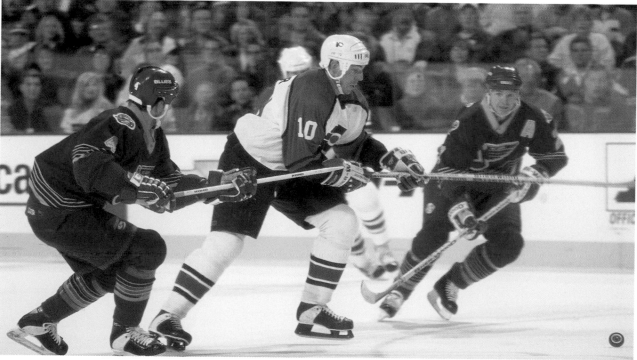

Yashin has emerged as one of the league's brightest stars. In 1998–99 he led the Senators to finish second overall in the Eastern Conference before suffering a disappointing first round playoff loss to the Buffalo Sabres.

Opposite: Alexei Yashin of the Ottawa Senators tries to hold off a Rangers defender while attempting a wraparound from behind the New York net.

Top: Alexei Yashin is sent flying as he is hit from behind.

Above: A gifted goal scorer in the 1998–99 season, Alexei Yashin finished second, behind Teemu Selanne, in the race for the first-ever Richard Trophy. The trophy, named after Montreal Canadiens legend Maurice "Rocket" Richard, is awarded to the player who scores the most goals during the regular season.

Right: Yashin extends himself to use his reach to keep the puck at a safe distance from the New York defender.

Opposite: Alexei Yashin of the Senators ties up Bobby Carpenter of the Devils as they fight for a face-off.

Mark Messier and Trevor Linden prepare to take the draw. The two would play together briefly as Vancouver Canucks before Linden's trade to the New York Islanders.

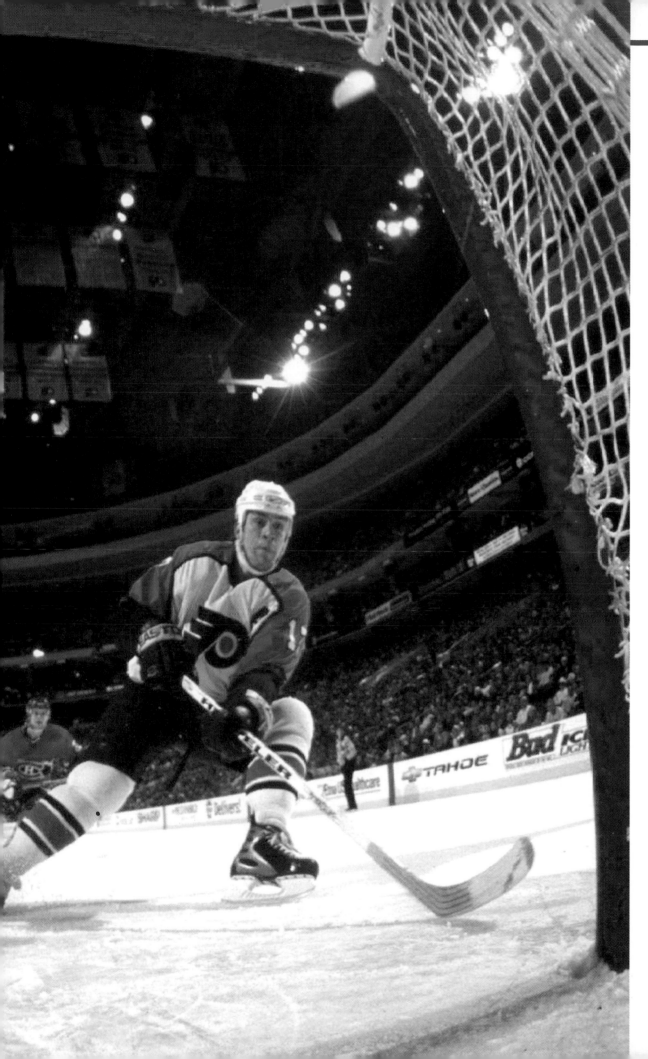

Left: Rod Brind'Amour beats the Montreal goaltender to the stick side.

Following pages:
Left: A Canadian fanatic.

Right: Many Canadians made the long trip to Nagano to show their support for Team Canada.

The Nagano Olympics

Manon Rheaume, the world's most famous female hockey player, played nets for Canada at the Olympics.

The American women's team celebrates after defeating Canada in the Gold Medal game. Nagano was the first Olympics in which women's hockey was an official sport.

271

Top left: Canada has always relied on a rugged physical style to counter the finesse games of the European teams at international tournaments.

Bottom left: Chris Pronger pounds Sweden's Daniel Alfredsson beside the Canadian net.

Opposite: Josef Beranek of the Czech Republic tangles with Teppo Nummienen of Finland.

Swedish star Mats Sundin flips a back-
hand past sprawling USA goaltender
Mike Richter. Sweden defeated the
Americans 4–2.

Never afraid to stray from his crease, Dominik Hasek plays the puck behind his net in order to impede the progress of Russia's Valeri Bure.

John LeClair leaps into the air in an effort to screen the view of Canadian goalie, Patrick Roy. One of the best to ever play the position, Roy had still never been selected to represent Canada in international competition before the 1998 Olympics.

Opposite: Dominik Hasek bites
his gold medal after leading the Czech
Republic to Olympic victory over
perennial powerhouses such as Canada,
the USA, and Sweden.

The World Cup 1996

The German goaltender, Josef Heiss, makes a diving stop on Canada's Trevor Linden at the 1996 World Cup.

Above: Team USA star, Brett Hull, hoists the World Cup after scoring the tying goal to defeat Canada in the final game.

Left: Eric Lindros and Mike Richter peer into the net following a Brendan Shanahan goal in Game Two of the World Cup final.

Opposite: Steve Yzerman tries to out-wait American goaltender Mike Richter in the 1996 World Cup finals.

Farewell to a Legend

Sunday April 18, 1999, marked the end of a sporting era. In New York's Madison Square Garden, Wayne Gretzky, the Great One, played his final NHL game.

A child phenom, Gretzky signed with the Indianapolis Racers of the WHA in 1978. Shortly after, he was sold to the Edmonton Oilers, where he would begin making hockey history. It was in Edmonton where the Great One was at his Greatest. Scoring at an unprecedented pace, Gretzky would smash many of the NHL's most impressive records and win four Stanley Cups as the leader of a young and incredibly talented Oilers team.

On August 9, 1988, hockey fans were shocked to learn that Gretzky had been traded, or as some would argue, sold again, this time to the Los Angeles Kings. In California he would never win the Stanley Cup, but he would lead the Kings to the finals in 1991, defeating his former teammates along the way. Gretzky continued to be a dominant force in the league and his popularity in

Los Angeles has been credited with giving the NHL the fan base it needed to expand into the American Sunbelt. In 1996, with the Kings facing financial difficulties, Gretzky was traded to St. Louis. Unable to reach a contract agreement with the Blues, he signed with the New York Rangers that summer.

Number 99 was enthusiastically embraced by the Madison Square Garden faithful and seemed energized by his reunion with his friend and former teammate Mark Messier. But Messier moved on to Vancouver just one season after Gretzky's arrival and the Rangers were unable to retool to challenge for the Cup. In 1998 Gretzky was granted his wish to pursue the one honor that had escaped him. The NHL decided to let its players

participate in the Nagano Olympics; unfortunately Team Canada went home out of the medals.

It is somehow fitting that Number 99 would choose to end his career in 1999. And choose he did. He was not forced out of the game by age or injuries. Gretzky is still a dangerous player. He chose to leave the game that he has defined in order to spend time with his young family and pursue his many business interests.

In the final analysis Gretzky retired from professional hockey the same way that he played it, with dignity, class, and a generous dose of excitement.

1999-2000 Playoffs

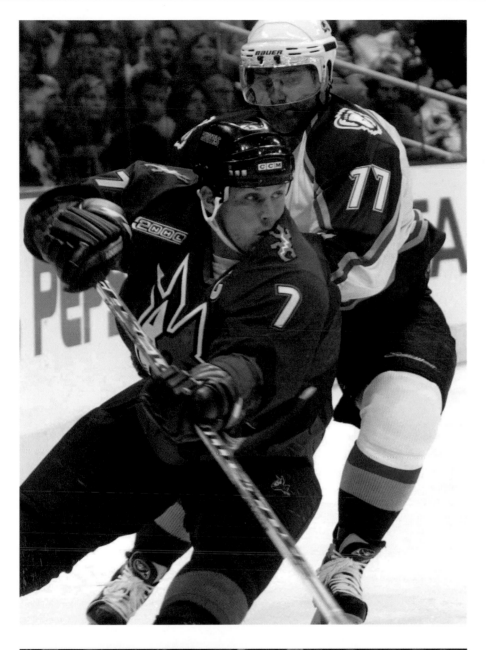

In the Western Conference, last year's champs, the Dallas Stars, battled the Colorado Avalanche to advance to the Stanley Cup finals again. The surprising Phoenix Coyotes made it to the quarterfinals but couldn't get past the formidable Avalanche. Detroit, St. Louis, San Jose, Edmonton and Los Angeles battled hard but were unable to make it into the Conference finals.

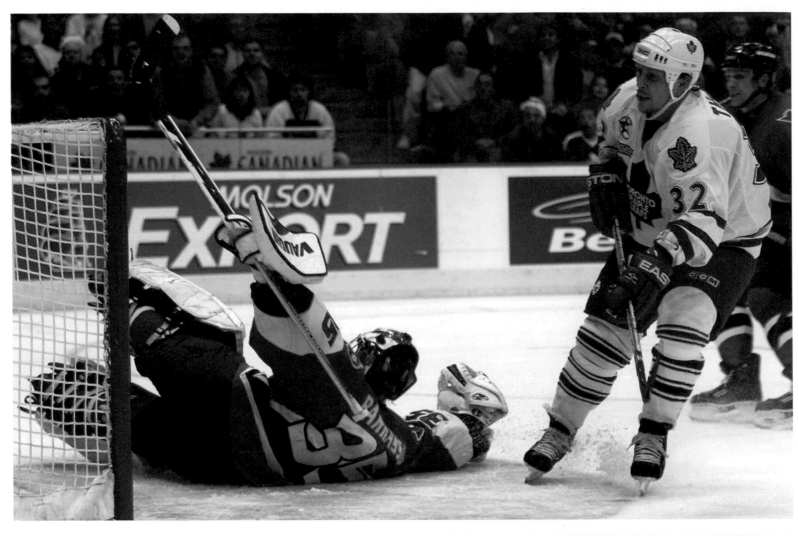

In the Eastern Conference, after beating the Pittsburgh Penguins and the Buffalo Sabres, the Philadelphia Flyers lost the Conference final in a hard fought battle against the New Jersey Devils. The Washington Capitals, Toronto Maple Leafs, Ottawa Senators and Florida Panthers all fell short in their playoff efforts this year.

This year's Stanley Cup finals pitted last season's champion Dallas Stars against 1995 Cup winners the New Jersey Devils. After falling behind in the series 3 games to 1, Dallas engaged in a valiant effort to defend their title as the Stanley Cup champs.

Tight defense and great goaltending by the Devils' Martin Brodeur kept the Stars at bay in the final game of the series. Jason Arnott's double-overtime goal in Game 6 secured the Devils' second Stanley Cup victory in five years.

Stanley Cup Winners
Since the formation of the NHL in1917

Year	W-L IN Finals	Winner	Coach	Finalist	Coach
2000	4-2	New Jersey	Larry Robinson	Dallas	Ken Hitchcock
1999	4-2	Dallas	Ken Hitchcock	Buffalo	Lindy Ruff
1998	4-0	Detroit	Scotty Bowman	Washington	Ron Wilson
1997	4-0	Detroit	Scotty Bowman	Philadelphia	Terry Murray
1996	4-0	Colorado	Marc Crawford	Florida	Doug MacLean
1995	4-0	New Jersey	Jacques Lemaire	Detroit	Scotty Bowman
1994	4-3	NY Rangers	Mike Keenan	Vancouver	Pat Quinn
1993	4-1	Montreal	Jacques Demers	Los Angeles	Barry Melrose
1992	4-0	Pittsburgh	Scotty Bowman	Chicago	Mike Keenan
1991	4-2	Pittsburgh	Bob Johnson	Minnesota	Bob Gainey
1990	4-1	Edmonton	John Muckler	Boston	Mike Milbury
1989	4-2	Calgary	Terry Crisp	Montreal	Pat Burns
1988	4-0	Edmonton	Glen Sather	Boston	Terry OiReilly
1987	4-3	Edmonton	Glen Sather	Philadelphia	Mike Keenan
1986	4-1	Montreal	Jean Perron	Calgary	Bob Johnson
1985	4-1	Edmonton	Glen Sather	Philadelphia	Mike Keenan
1984	4-1	Edmonton	Glen Sather	NY Islanders	Al Arbour
1983	4-0	NY Islanders	Al Arbour	Edmonton	Glen Sather
1982	4-0	NY Islanders	Al Arbour	Vancouver	Roger Neilson
1981	4-1	NY Islanders	Al Arbour	Minnesota	Glen Sonmor
1980	4-2	NY Islanders	Al Arbour	Philadelphia	Pat Quinn
1979	4-1	Montreal	Scotty Bowman	NY Rangers	Fred Shero
1978	4-2	Montreal	Scotty Bowman	Boston	Don Cherry
1977	4-0	Montreal	Scotty Bowman	Boston	Don Cherry
1976	4-0	Montreal	Scotty Bowman	Philadelphia	Fred Shero
1975	4-2	Philadelphia	Fred Shero	Buffalo	Floyd Smith
1974	4-2	Philadelphia	Fred Shero	Boston	Bep Guidolin
1973	4-2	Montreal	Scotty Bowman	Chicago	Billy Reay
1972	4-2	Boston	Tom Johnson	NY Rangers	Emile Francis
1971	4-3	Montreal	Al MacNeil	Chicago	Billy Reay
1970	4-0	Boston	Harry Sinden	St. Louis	Scotty Bowman
1969	4-0	Montreal	Claude Ruel	St. Louis	Scotty Bowman
1968	4-0	Montreal	Toe Blake	St. Louis	Scotty Bowman
1967	4-2	Toronto	Punch Imlach	Montreal	Toe Blake
1966	4-2	Montreal	Toe Blake	Detroit	Sid Abel
1965	4-3	Montreal	Toe Blake	Chicago	Billy Reay
1964	4-3	Toronto	Punch Imlach	Detroit	Sid Abel
1963	4-1	Toronto	Punch Imlach	Detroit	Sid Abel
1962	4-2	Toronto	Punch Imlach	Chicago	Rudy Pilous
1961	4-2	Chicago	Rudy Pilous	Detroit	Sid Abel
1960	4-3	Montreal	Toe Blake	Toronto	Punch Imlach
1959	4-1	Montreal	Toe Blake	Toronto	Punch Imlach
1958	4-2	Montreal	Toe Blake	Boston	Milt Schmidt
1957	4-1	Montreal	Toe Blake	Boston	Milt Schmidt
1956	4-1	Montreal	Toe Blake	Detroit	Jimmy Skinner

Year	W-L IN Finals	Winner	Coach	Finalist	Coach
1955	4-3	Detroit	Jimmy Skinner	Montreal	Dick Irvin
1954	4-3	Detroit	Tommy Ivan	Montreal	Dick Irvin
1953	4-1	Montreal	Dick Irvin	Boston	Lynn Patrick
1952	4-0	Detroit	Tommy Ivan	Montreal	Dick Irvin
1951	4-1	Toronto	Joe Primeau	Montreal	Dick Irvin
1950	4-3	Detroit	Tommy Ivan	NY Rangers	Lynn Patrick
1949	4-0	Toronto	Hap Day	Detroit	Tommy Ivan
1948	4-0	Toronto	Hap Day	Detroit	Tommy Ivan
1947	4-2	Toronto	Hap Day	Montreal	Dick Irvin
1946	4-1	Montreal	Dick Irvin	Boston	Dit Clapper
1945	4-3	Toronto	Hap Day	Detroit	Jack Adams
1944	4-0	Montreal	Dick Irvin	Chicago	Paul Thompson
1943	4-0	Detroit	Jack Adams	Boston	Art Ross
1942	4-3	Toronto	Hap Day	Detroit	Jack Adams
1941	4-0	Boston	Cooney Weiland	Detroit	Ebbie Goodfellow
1940	4-2	NY Rangers	Frank Boucher	Toronto	Dick Irvin
1939	4-1	Boston	Art Ross	Toronto	Dick Irvin
1938	3-1	Chicago	Bill Stewart	Toronto	Dick Irvin
1937	3-2	Detroit	Jack Adams	NY Rangers	Lester Patrick
1936	3-1	Detroit	Jack Adams	Toronto	Dick Irvin
1935	3-0	Mtl. Maroons	Tommy Gorman	Toronto	Dick Irvin
1934	3-1	Chicago	Tommy Gorman	Detroit	Herbie Lewis
1933	3-1	NY Rangers	Lester Patrick	Toronto	Dick Irvin
1932	3-0	Toronto	Dick Irvin	NY Rangers	Lester Patrick
1931	3-2	Montreal	Cecil Hart	Chicago	Dick Irvin
1930	2-0	Montreal	Cecil Hart	Boston	Art Ross
1929	2-0	Boston	Cy Denneny	NY Rangers	Lester Patrick
1928	3-2	NY Rangers	Lester Patrick	Mtl. Maroons	Eddie Gerard
1927	2-0-2	Ottawa	Dave Gill	Boston	Art Ross
The National Hockey League assumed control of Stanley Cup competition after 1926					
1926	3-1	Mtl. Maroons	Eddie Gerard	Victoria	
1925	3-1	Victoria	Lester Patrick	Montreal	
1924	2-0	Montreal	Leo Dandurand	Cgy. Tigers	
	2-0			Van. Maroons	
1923	2-0	Ottawa	Pete Green	Edm. Eskimos	
	3-1			Van. Maroons	
1922	3-2	Tor. St. Pats	Eddie Powers	Van. Millionaires	
1921	3-2	Ottawa	Pete Green	Van. Millionaires	
1920	3-2	Ottawa	Pete Green	Seattle	
1919	2-2-1	No decision – series between Montreal and Seattle cancelled due to influenza epidemic			
1918	3-2	Tor. Arenas	Dick Carroll	Van. Millionaires	

Art Ross Trophy
Scoring leader

2000	Jaromir Jagr, Pit.
1999	Jaromir Jagr, Pit.
1998	Jaromir Jagr, Pit.
1997	Mario Lemieux, Pit.
1996	Mario Lemieux, Pit.
1995	Jaromir Jagr, Pit.
1994	Wayne Gretzky, L.A.
1993	Mario Lemieux, Pit.
1992	Mario Lemieux, Pit.
1991	Wayne Gretzky, L.A.
1990	Wayne Gretzky, L.A.
1989	Mario Lemieux, Pit.
1988	Mario Lemieux, Pit.
1987	Wayne Gretzky, L.A.
1986	Wayne Gretzky, Edm.
1985	Wayne Gretzky, Edm.
1984	Wayne Gretzky, Edm.
1983	Wayne Gretzky, Edm.
1982	Wayne Gretzky, Edm.
1981	Wayne Gretzky, Edm.
1980	Marcel Dionne, L.A.
1979	Bryan Trottier, NYI
1978	Guy LaFleur, Mtl.
1977	Guy LaFleur, Mtl.
1976	Guy LaFleur, Mtl.
1975	Bobby Orr, Bos.
1974	Phil Esposito, Bos.
1973	Phil Esposito, Bos.
1972	Phil Esposito, Bos.
1971	Phil Esposito, Bos.
1970	Bobby Orr, Bos.
1969	Phil Esposito, Bos.
1968	Stan Mikita, Chi.
1967	Stan Mikita, Chi.
1966	Bobby Hull, Chi.
1965	Stan Mikita, Chi.
1964	Stan Mikita, Chi.
1963	Gordie Howe, Det.
1962	Bobby Hull, Chi.
1961	Bernie Geoffrion, Mtl.
1960	Bobby Hull, Chi.
1959	Dickie Moore, Mtl.

Hart Trophy
Most valuable player

2000	Chris Pronger, St. L.
1999	Jaromir Jagr, Pit.
1998	Dominik Hasek, Buf.
1997	Dominik Hasek, Buf.
1996	Mario Lemieux, Pit.
1995	Eric Lindros, Phi.
1994	Sergei Fedorov, Det.
1993	Mario Lemieux, Pit.
1992	Mark Messier, NYR
1991	Brett Hull, St. L.
1990	Mark Messier, Edm.
1989	Wayne Gretzky, L.A.
1988	Mario Lemieux, Pit.
1987	Wayne Gretzky, Edm.
1986	Wayne Gretzky, Edm.
1985	Wayne Gretzky, Edm.
1984	Wayne Gretzky, Edm.
1983	Wayne Gretzky, Edm
1982	Wayne Gretzky, Edm.
1981	Wayne Gretzky, Edm.
1980	Wayne Gretzky, Edm.
1979	Bryan Trottier, NYI
1978	Guy LaFleur, Mtl.
1977	Guy LaFleur, Mtl.
1976	Bobby Clarke, Phi.
1975	Bobby Clarke, Phi.
1974	Phil Esposito, Bos.
1973	Bobby Clarke, Phi.
1972	Bobby Orr, Bos.
1971	Bobby Orr, Bos.
1970	Bobby Orr, Bos.
1969	Phil Esposito, Bos.
1968	Stan Mikita, Chi.
1967	Stan Mikita, Chi.
1966	Bobby Hull, Chi.
1965	Bobby Hull, Chi.
1964	Jean Beliveau, Mtl.
1963	Gordie Howe, Det.
1962	Jacques Plante, Mtl.
1961	Bernie Geoffrion, Mtl.
1960	Gordie Howe, Det.
1959	Andy Bathgate, NYR

Vezina Trophy
Best goaltender

2000	Olag Kolzig, Wash.
1999	Dominik Hasek, Buf.
1998	Dominik Hasek, Buf.
1997	Dominik Hasek, Buf.
1996	Jim Carey, Wsh.
1995	Dominik Hasek, Buf.
1994	Dominik Hasek, Buf.
1993	Ed Belfour, Chi.
1992	Patrick Roy, Mtl.
1991	Ed Belfour, Chi.
1990	Patrick Roy, Mtl.
1989	Patrick Roy, Mtl.
1988	Grant Fuhr, Edm.
1987	Ron Hextall, Phi.
1986	John Vanbiesbrouck, NYR
1985	Pelle Lindbergh, Phi.
1984	Tom Barrasso, Buf.
1983	Pete Peeters, Bos.
1982	Billy Smith, NYI.
1981	Richard Sevigny, Mtl.
	Denis Herron, Mtl.
	Michel Larocque, Mtl.
1980	Bob Sauve, Buf.
	Don Edwards, Buf.
1979	Ken Dryden, Mtl.
	Michel Larocque, Mtl.
1978	Ken Dryden, Mtl.
	Michel Larocque, Mtl.
1977	Ken Dryden, Mtl.
	Michel Larocque, Mtl.
1976	Ken Dryden, Mtl.
1975	Bernie Parent, Phi.
1974	Bernie Parent, Phi. (tie)
	Tony Esposito, Chi. (tie)
1973	Ken Dryden, Mtl.
1972	Tony Esposito, Chi.
	Gary Smith, Chi.
1971	Ed Giacomin, NYR
	Gilles Villemure, NYR
1970	Tony Esposito, Chi.
1969	Jacques Plante, St.L.
	Glenn Hall, St.L.

Art Ross Trophy
Scoring leader

1958	Dickie Moore, Mtl.
1957	Gordie Howe, Det.
1956	Jean Beliveau, Mtl.
1955	Bernie Geoffrion, Mtl.
1954	Gordie Howe, Det.
1953	Gordie Howe, Det.
1952	Gordie Howe, Det.
1951	Gordie Howe, Det.
1950	Ted Lindsay, Det.
1949	Roy Conacher, Chi.
1948 *	Elmer Lach, Mtl.
1947	Max Bentley, Chi.
1946	Max Bentley, Chi.
1945	Elmer Lach, Mtl.
1944	Herb Cain, Bos.
1943	Doug Bentley, Chi.
1942	Bryan Hextall, NYR
1941	Bill Cowley, Bos.
1940	Milt Schmidt, Bos.
1939	Toe Blake, Mtl.
1938	Gordie Drillon, Tor.
1937	Dave Schriner, NYA
1936	Dave Schriner, NYA
1935	Charlie Conacher, Tor.
1934	Charlie Conacher, Tor.
1933	Bill Cook, NYR
1932	Harvey Jackson, Tor.
1931	Howie Morenz, Mtl.
1930	Cooney Weiland, Bos.
1929	Ace Bailey, Tor.
1928	Howie Morenz, Mtl.
1927	Bill Cook, NYR
1926	Nels Stewart, Mtl. M.
1925	Babe Dye, Tor.
1924	Cy Denneny, Ott.
1923	Babe Dye, Tor.
1922	Punch Broadbent, Ott.
1921	Newsy Lalond, Mtl.
1920	Joe Malone, Que.
1919	Newsy Lalond, Mtl.
1918	Joe Malone, Que.

Hart Trophy
Most valuable player

1958	Gordie Howe, Det.
1957	Gordie Howe, Det.
1956	Jean Beliveau, Mtl.
1955	Ted Kennedy, Tor.
1954	Al Rollins, Chi.
1953	Gordie Howe, Det.
1952	Gordie Howe, Det.
1951	Milt Schmidt, Bos.
1950	Chuck Rayner, NYR
1949	Sid Abel, Det.
1948	Buddy O'Connor, NYR
1947	Maurice Richard, Mtl.
1946	Max Bentley, Chi.
1945	Elmer Lach, Mtl.
1944	Babe Pratt, Tor.
1943	Bill Cowley, Bos.
1942	Tom Anderson, Bos.
1941	Bill Cowley, Bos.
1940	Ebbie Goodfellow, Det.
1939	Toe Blake, Mtl.
1938	Eddie Shore, Bos.
1937	Babe Siebert, Mtl.
1936	Eddie Shore, Bos.
1935	Eddie Shore, Bos.
1934	Aurel Joliat, Mtl.
1933	Eddie Shore, Bos.
1932	Howie Morenz, Mtl.
1931	Howie Morenz, Mtl.
1930	Nels Stewart, Mtl.M.
1929	Roy Worters, NYA
1928	Howie Morenz, Mtl.
1927	Herb Gardiner, Mtl.
1926	Nels Stewart, Mtl.M.
1925	Billy Burch, Ham.
1924	Frank Nighbor, Ott.

Vezina Trophy
Best goaltender

1968	Gump Worsley, Mtl.
	Rogatien Vachon, Mtl.
1967	Glenn Hall, Chi.
	Denis Dejordy, Chi.
1966	Gump Worsley, Mtl.
	Charlie Hodge, Mtl.
1965	Terry Sawchuk, Tor.
	Johnny Bower, Tor.
1964	Charlie Hodge, Mtl.
1963	Glenn Hall, Chi.
1962	Jacques Plante, St.L.
1961	Johnny Bower, Tor.
1960	Jacques Plante, St.L.
1959	Jacques Plante, St.L.
1958	Jacques Plante, St.L.
1957	Jacques Plante, St.L.
1956	Jacques Plante, St.L.
1955	Terry Sawchuk, Det.
1954	Harry Lumley, Tor.
1953	Terry Sawchuk, Det.
1952	Terry Sawchuk, Det.
1951	Al Rollins, Tor.
1950	Bill Durnan, Mtl.
1949	Bill Durnan, Mtl.
1948	Turk Broda, Tor.
1947	Bill Durnan, Mtl.
1946	Bill Durnan, Mtl.
1945	Bill Durnan, Mtl.
1944	Bill Durnan, Mtl.
1943	Johnny Mowers, Det.
1942	Frank Brimsek, Bos
1941	Turk Broda, Tor.
1940	Dave Kerr, NYR
1939	Frank Brimsek, Bos.
1938	Tiny Thompson, Bos.
1937	Normie Smith, Det.
1936	Tiny Thompson, Bos.
1935	Lorne Chabot, Chi.
1934	Charlie Gardner, Chi.

Index

Note: Italicized numbers refer to captions.

Abel, Sid, 40, *43*, 44
Ahearne, J.F. (Bunny), 29, 30
Air Canada Centre (Toronto), *204*, 205
Albelin, Tommy, 220
Alfredsson, Daniel, *273*
Anaheim Mighty Ducks, 202
Anderson, Glenn, *57*, 179
American Basketball Association, 117
Apps, Syl, 40, *40*
Arbour, Al, 141, *141*, 200
Art Ross Trophy, 43, 65, 91
Ascent Entertainment, 204
Atlanta Knights, 215
Aubut, Marcel, 204, 209

Baby Bulls, 103
Badali, Gus, 159
Bailey, Irvin (Ace), 34, *35*
Ballard, Harold, 79
Barber, Bill, 104
Barilko, Bill, 79, *82*
Barrasso, Tom, 200
Bathgate, Andy, 63
Battle of Pennsylvania, 194
Bauer, Bobby, 34, 36, *38*, 40
Baun, Bobby, 73, *75*
Beliveau, Jean, *54*, *55*, *56*, *57*, 86, 113
Benedict, Clint, 26, *26*
Bennett, Harvey, 57
Bentley, Doug, 38, *39*
Bentley, Max, 38, *39*
Beraneck, Josef, *273*
Berlinguette, Louis, 19
Berry, Bob, 151
Bertuzzi, Larry, 209
Bettman, Gary, 83, 211
Binkley, Les, 84
Birmingham Bulls, 103
   (*See also* Baby Bulls)
Black Hawks. *See* Chicago Blackhawks
Blair, Andy, 35
Blake, Toe, 40, *40*, 54, *54*, *58*, 60,
   60, 63, 72, 76, 86, 113, 200
Bossy, Mike, 117, 141, *146*, *148*, 181
Boston Bruins, 14, 26, 31, 33, 34, *35*, 35,
   36, 38, 40, *47*, *55*, *57*, 58, 64, 68, 69, 72,
   76, 84,   87, 88, 89, *90*, *91*, *97*, 103, 112,
   123, *127*, *135*, *146*, 150, 166, 176, 178, *187*,
   216
Boston Garden, 64, 86, 88, 168, *207*
Bouchard, Pierre, 116, 121
Boucher, Frank, 38
Bourne, Bob, 150, *152*
Bourque, Ray, *178*
Bower, Johnny, *43*, *51*, *70*, 72
Bowman, Scotty, 60, 86, *102*, 110, 116,
   117, 121, 199-200
Boyle, Joe, 11, 13
Brandon Wheat Kings, 14
Brimsek, Frank, 40
Brind'Amour, Rod, *267*
British Hockey Association, 29
"Broad Street Bullies," 104, *105*, *108*, 110,
   113, 116, *185*
   (*See also* Philadelphia Flyers)

Broda, Turk, 39, 40, *40*
Brodeur, Martin, *217*, 220
Brooklyn Americans, 36, *38*
(*See also* New York Americans)
Brown, Arnie, *122*
Bruneteau, Modere (Mud), 35
Bucyk, Johnny, 89
Buffalo, Sabres, 118, 121, 199, 200, *226*,
   245, *247*, *260*, *291*
Bure, Pavel, 214, *221*
Bure, Valeri, *275*
Burke, Richard, 204
Byng, Lady, *20*, 21
   (*See also* Lady Byng Trophy)

Calder Trophy, 164
Calgary Flames, 119, *127*, *151*, 163, 164,
   164, 165, 166, *166*, 170, 172, 173, 176,
   178, 203, 219, 220, 247
Cameron, Jack, 29
Campbell, Clarence, 49, 58, *58*, 79, 83,
   83, 103
Canada Cup, 161, 164-65, *163*, *176*, 198,
   199, 209, 214
Canadian Airlines Saddledome, 205
Canadian Amateur Hockey Association,
28, 29
Canadiens, les, 29, *23*
   (*See also* Montreal Canadiens)
Canadiens Seniors, 50
Carbonneau, Guy, 165
Carling O'Keefe Breweries, 204
Carpenter, Bobby, *262*
Carroll, Bill, 142, 148
Carson, Jimmy, 168, 176
Cashman, Wayne, 89, 112
Chabot, Lorne, 14, 35, *35*
Chartraw, Rick, 116
Cheevers, Gerry, 89, *90*, 103
Chelios, Chris, *170*
Chicago Blackhawks, *13*, 36, 38, 50, 58,
   63, 64, *64*, 65, 68, 72, 73, 97, 102, 150,
   151, 154, 172, 256
Chicago Stadium, 63, *206*, 208
Civic Arena (Pittsburgh), 159
Clancy, King, 32, *32*, 33
Clapper, Dit, 40
Clarke, Bobby, 84, *85*, *96*, 104, *108*,
   110, 112-13, *146*
Clark, Wendel, *250*, 255
Cleveland Crusaders, 103
Cobb, Ty, 22
Coffey, Paul, *57*, *193*, *237*
Coleman, Jim, 26, 28
Coliseum (Vancouver), 205
Collier's (magazine), 34
Colorado Avalanche, 203, *203*, 219, 222,
   231, *232*, 292
   (*See also* Quebec Nordiques)
Colorado Rockies, 110, *127*
Columbus Blue Jackets, 202
Colville, Mac, 36, 38
Colville, Neil, 36, 38
Conacher, Charlie, 33, *35*
Conacher, Lionel, *13*
Conn Smythe Trophy, *110*, *133*, *146*, 168,
   187, 199, *217*, 220, *232*
Consentino, Frank, 22
Copps Coliseum (Hamilton), 155

Corel Centre (Ottawa), 205
Cournoyer, Yvan, *88*, *95*, *101*, 113,
   119, *135*
Cowley, Bill, 40
Craig, Jim, 163
Craven, Murray, 216
Creamery Kings, 18
Crichton, Kyle, 34
Crisp, Terry, *176*
Cullen, John, 195
Czech Republic (team), *273*, *275*

Daigle, Alexandre, 209
Dallas Stars, 119, *246*, *247*, 292, 294, 296
Dandurand, Leo, 25
Davidson, Bill, 203-4
Davidson, Bob, 48, 50, 54
Davidson, Gary, 102
Delecchio, Alex, *45*
Denver Nuggets, 117
Detroit Olympia, *207*
Detroit Pistons, 203
Detroit Red Wings, 36, 38, 40, *43*, 43, 44,
   45, 54, 58, 73, 76, 164, 171, 176, 200,
   200, 202-3, 205, 215, *215*, 222, 236, 240
Dineen, Bill, 104
Dineen, Kevin, 210
Dominion Hockey Challenge Cup, 11
Doraty, Ken, 35
Dryden, Dave, 133
Dryden, Ken, 92, *92*, *101*, 116, 117, 119,
   121, *127*, 133
Duchesne, Steve, 209
Dumart, Woody, 34, 36, *38*, 40
Dupont, André (Moose), 104, *105*, *106*,
   108, 110, 112
Durnan, Bill, 35, 40, *40*

Eagleson, Alan, 60, 95, 113, 119,
   178-79, 195, *210*, 210
Eastern Canada Hockey Association, 17
Eastern Conference, *255*, *260*
Eastern Canada Hockey League, 26
Edmonton Eskimos, 28
Edmonton Oilers, *57*, 103, 104, 117, 119,
   138, *139*, 140-41, 142, 150, 151, 154,
   155, 157-59, *158*, 164-66, *166*, 168,
   171-72, 176, 178, 179, 185, *187*, *191*, *192*,
   193, 216, *217*, 220, *283*
Einstein, Albert, 26
Englblom, Brian, 150
Eruzione, Mike, 163
Esposito, Phil, 86, 88, 89, 95, 104,
   112, 155
Esposito, Tony, *64*, *97*, 133
Expo 67, 84

Federov, Sergei, *200*, 202, 236
Ferguson, John, 68
Fetisov, Slava (Viacheslav), 163, 164,
   200, *200*, 202
Fischler, Stan, 141
Fisher, Red, 121
Flammen, Fernie, 76
Fletcher, Cliff, 164
Fleury, Theo, *173*, *205*, 220
Florida Panthers, 217, 219, 221
Flying Frenchmen, 19
Forsberg, Peter, 209, 221, 225, 226, 229,

231, 232
Fortier, Marius, 102-3
Foster, Jimmy, 30
Fournier, Jacques, 19
Francis, Emile, 64, 68
Frank J. Selke Trophy, *85*, 200
Fredrickson, Frank, 24, 25-26, *25*, 28
Ftorek, Robbie, 172
Fuhr, Grant, *57*, 158, *158*, 165, 168, *168*,
   192, *250*

Gadsby, Bill, 73
Gagnon, Johnny, 23, 25
Gainey, Bob, 116, 117, 119, 165
Game, The (Dryden), 92
Gardiner, Charlie, 30
Garner, Andrew, 11
Gardner, Jimmy, 17
Garvey, Ed, 178
Gauthier, Pierre, 202
Gazette, The (Montreal), 121
Gelinas, Martin, 168, 176
Geoffrion, Bernard (Boom Boom), *56*,
   57, 113
Gillie, Clark, *108*, 141, *146*, *148*, 150,
   152, 181
Gilmour, Doug, *170*, 172, *214*
GM Place, 205
Gonchar, Sergei, *258*
Goodenow, Bob, *210*, 211, 214
Goring, Butch, 142, *146*, *148*
Goulet, Michel, 103
Granato, Cammi, 215
Graves, Adam, 176, *237*
Green, Rick, 150
Gretzky, Wayne, *57*, 103, 117, 140-41, *140*,
   155, *155*, 157, 159, 163, 166, 168, *168*,
   171-72, *171*, 176, *176*, 178, 179, *187*, *190*,
   191, 198, *198*, 208, *217*, 219, *219*
Grey, Earl, 22
Griffiths, Arthur, 176, 178
Grundman, Irving, 121, 150, 151

Habitants, 20, 24
Hall, Bad Joe, 21
Hall, Glenn, 76, *91*, 92
Hart, Cecil, 25
Hart Trophy, 21, 43, *65*, *85*, *197*, 200,
   202, 222, 234, 247
Hartford Whalers, *46*, 103, 104, 210
Harvey, Doug , *57*, 58, *87*, *87*, 113
Hasek, Dominik, 200, 202, 214, 220,
   245, *247*, *275*, *276*
Hatskin, Ben, 102
Heiss, Josef, *279*
Henderson, Paul, *94*, 95, *97*, *101*
Henry, "Sugar Jim," 47
Hewitt, Foster, *31*, 32, 35
Hextall, Bryan, 38
Hextall, Ron, 209, *209*
Hiller, Dutch, 57
Hindy, Kelly, *156*
Hockey Hall of Fame, *31*, *36*, *40*, *57*, 64,
   68, 73, 121, 178, 185, 204
Hockey News, 195
Hodge, Ken, 89, 112
Horner, Red, 33
Hotchkiss, Harley, 208
Houle, Réjean, 119

Housley, Phil, 200
Houston Aeros, 103
Howe, Gordie, 40, 43-46, *43, 45, 46,* 103-4, 155, *168,* 220
Howe, Mark, 103, *103*
Howe, Marty, 103, *103*
Huffman, Kerry, 209
Hughes, Jack, 29
Hull, Bobby, *45,* 63-64, *64, 65,* 68, 86, 95, 102
Hull, Brett, *246, 247, 281, 294, 296*
Hutchison, Bruce, 22

Igloo (Pittsburgh), 208
Imlach, Punch, *61,* 72
Indianapolis Racers, 103, *283*
International American Hockey League, 26
International Hockey League, 215
International Ice Hockey Federation, 30

Jackson, Don, *166*
Jackson, Busher, 33, *35*
Jagr, Jaromir, *195,* 198, 221, *234*
James, Graham, 195
Jarvis, Doug, 119, 150
Jenish, D'Arcy, 10, 13
Johnson, Bob, 164, 199
Johnson, Mark, 163
Joliat, Aurel, 23, *23,* 25
Journal de Montréal, Le, 121

Kallur, Anders, 150, *152*
Kapustin, Sergei, 163
Kariya, Paul, 221
Keenan, Mike, 216
Kelly, Dave, 110
Kelly, Red, 87
Kennedy, Ted, *39,* 40, 45
Keon, Dave, *78,* 79
Kharlamov, Valeri, *95, 96,* 113
Kid Line, 33, *35*
Kilpatrick, John, 217
Kimberly Dynamiters, 31
Klatt, Trent, *237*
Klima, Petr, 176
KLM Line, 164
Koharski, Don, 176
Korolev, Igor, *256*
Kozlov, Slava, 200, *200,* 202
Kraut Line, 34, 36, *38*
Krushelnyski, Mike, 168, 190
Krutov, Vladimir, 164
Kurri, Jari, *57,* 179

L.A. Lakers, 219
Lach, Elmer, 40, *40,* 57
Lacroix, André, 84
Lady Byng Trophy, *20, 21, 65, 146*
Lafleur, Guy, 116, *118,* 119-20, *131,* 142
Lalonde, Newsy, 17, *17,* 50
Langevin, Dave, 158
Langway, Rod, 150
Lapointe, Guy, 116, 119, 121
Larionov, Igor, 164, 200, *200,* 202
Larouche, Pierre, 112-13
Laughlin, Craig, 150
Laviolette, Jack, 19
Laycoe, Hal, 58

Leach, Reggie, 84, *106*
LeClair, John, *217, 258, 275*
Leetch, Brian, *217*
Legends of Hockey (documentary), 11
Legion of Doom Line, *258*
Lemaire, Jacques, 116, 119, 121, *135*
Lemieux, Claude, *166,* 232
Lemieux, Mario, 159, *159, 176,* 194-95, *194, 195, 197,* 198-99, 208, 221
Lindbergh, Pelle, *160, 161, 161*
Linden, Trevor, *265, 279*
Lindros, Eric, *205,* 208-9, *208, 222, 231, 258, 281*
Lindsay, Ted, 40, *43, 44,* 58
Lindstrom, Willy, *185*
Linseman, Ken, 103
Los Angeles Kings, *45,* 119, *128,* 150, *168, 168,* 171-72, *176, 178, 178,* 200, 202, 219, *283, 285*

McClelland, Kevin, 176
McCool, Frank, 54
McDonald, Lanny, *127, 164*
McEwan, Mike, 142
McGee, D'Arcy, 13
McGee, Frank, 13
McGwire, Mark, 220
MacInnis, Al, 172
McKay, Doug, 176
McLaren, Kyle, *216*
Maclean's magazine, 22
MacLeish, Rick, 104, 112
McNall, Bruce, 171, 195
McSorley, Marty, *168, 171,* 219
MacTavish, Craig, *190*
McVeigh, Rabbit, 33
Macoun, Jamie, *166*
Madison Square Garden, 16, 31, 63, *207,* 217, *283, 285*
Mahovlich, Frank, 60, 76, *76*
Mahovlich, Pete, 116
Makarov, Sergei, 164
Malone, Joe, 54
Man and His World. *See* Expo 67
Maple Leaf Gardens (Toronto), *31,* 32, 34, *37,* 73, 76, 79, 205, 206, 208
Marine Midland Arena (Buffalo), *226*
Mellanby, Scott, 217, 219
Messier, Mark, *57,* 117, *176,* 178, 179, *187,* 216-17, *265, 285*
Metz, Nick, 54
Miami Arena, 219
Miami Screaming Eagles, 102, *110,* 112
Mikita, Stan, 63, 64, *65,* 68
Minnesota North Stars, *56, 105,* 142, *148, 154,* 157, 163, *181,* 199
"Miracle on Ice, The," 161, *162,* 214
Minnesota Wild, 202
Modano, Mike, *246, 247*
Mogilny, Alexander, *202*
Molson Centre (Montreal), 205
Molson, David, *60*
Montreal Amateur Athletic Association, 11
Montreal Canadiens, 14, 17, 19, *19,* 20, 21, 23, 24, *24,* 25, 36, 38, 40, *40, 43, 45,* 46, 48, 49, 50, 54, *54,* 57-58, 60, 64, 68, 72-73, 76, 79, 82, 86, 88, 92, 95, 103, *106,* 110, 112, 113-14, 116-17, 119-21, *123,*

127, 128, 133, 135, 137, 142, 150-51, *156, 157,* 163, *165, 166,* 172, *173* (*See also* Flying Frenchmen; Habitants)
Montreal Forum, 25, 48, 54, *57, 58, 59,* 95, 102, 159, 205, *206,* 208
Montreal Maroons, *13, 26, 28, 30,* 35, 36, *38*
Montreal Shamrocks, 22
Montreal Star, 121
Montreal Wanderers, 13, 19
Moore, Dickie, *57, 76,* 79, 113
Morenz, Howie, 23-25, *23, 24, 25,* 26
Morrow, Ken, 158
Mosienko, Bill, 38, *39*
Mullen, Joey, 164, *164, 165,* 172
Munro, Dunc, 28-29
Murphy, Joe, 176
Murphy, Larry, *176,* 198
Murray, Derik, 11
Murzyn, Dana, 178
Mutual Street Arena (Toronto), 32

Nagano (Olympics), *270-78, 287*
Naslund, Mats, 172
Nassau County Coliseum, 158
National Basketball Association, 203, 211, 214
National Football League, 178
National Hockey League Players Association (NHLPA), 58, 60, 178, 195, 210-11
New Jersey Devils, 119, *135, 155,* 163, *176, 187, 193, 217, 256,* 262
New York Americans, *23,* 31, 34, 35, 36
New York Islanders, *57,* 108, 117, *127,* 138, 141-42, *142-48,* 148-50, 151, *152,* 154, *154, 156,* 157-58, 164, *181, 185, 187, 191, 192,* 216, 225, *246,* 265
New York Raiders, 102
New York Rangers, 14, *14,* 16, 25, 31, 36, 38, 60, *70,* 73, 122, 142, 157, 163, 171, *185,* 209, 215-17, *216, 217,* 232, 237, *260, 262, 285*
New Westminster Royals, 17 (*See also* Portland Rosebuds)
Nighbor, Frank, *20,* 21
Nilan, Chris, 165
Norris Trophy, 185
Northlands Coliseum (Edmonton), 205 (*See also* Skyreach Centre)
1972 Summit Series, 94, 95, *96-102, 133*
Nuggets, 11, 13
Nummienen, Teppo, *273*
Nyrop, Bill, 121

Oakland Seals, 84
O'Brien, J. Ambrose, 14, 17, 18-19
O'Brien, Michael J., 14, 17-18, 19
Olympic Saddledome. *See* Canadian Airlines Saddledome
Omaha Knights, 73
Original Six, 36, 38, 40, 43, 44, 45, *57,* 63, 64, 73, 76, 79, 84, 86, 206-7, 208, 256
Original 21, 202
Orlando, Jimmy, *33*
Orr, Bobby, 64, 68, 69, 72, 87-89, *88, 91, 92,* 95, 112, 120, 122, 123, *125, 127,* 198

Oshawa Generals, *69*
Ottawa Arena, 205
Ottawa Senators, 21, *21,* 22, 32, 202, 205, 209, *260, 262*
Ozolinsh, Sandis, *232*

Pacific Coast Hockey Association, 14
Pacific Coast Hockey League, 26
Palace of Auburn Hills, 204
Palffy, Ziggy, 221
Parent, Bernie, 84, 102, 104, 110, *110,* 112, 113, 161
Parizeau, Jacques, 204
Patrick, Craig, 14, 199
Patrick, Dick, 14
Patrick, Frank, 12, 14, 16-17, 20, *21,* 22, 26
Patrick, Joseph, 16
Patrick, Lester, *12,* 14, 16-17, 18, 21, 22-23, 24, 25, 26, 31, 38
Patrick, Lynn, 14, 38
Patrick, Muzz, 14, 38
Persson, Stefan, 141, 142, *142,* 158
Petrov, Vladimir, 95
Philadelphia Blazers, 102, 103, *110*
Philadelphia Flyers, 84, *85,* 104, *108,* 110, *110,* 112-13, 116, 142, *146,* 150, 159, *160,* 161, 163, 165, *185, 187,* 194, 209, *217, 222, 231, 237, 241, 253*
Philadelphia Spectrum, 104, 194
Phoenix Coyotes, 104, 203
Pitre, Didier, 19
Pittsburgh Civic Arena, 159
Pittsburgh Penguins, 14, 86, 112, *142,* 159, *159, 181,* 194-95, *195, 197,* 198-200, 202, 221, 234
Pittsburgh Pirates, 25
Plante, Jacques, 26, *26,* 49, 57, 58, 60, 62, 63, 87, 112, 113, *128*
Plett, Willi, 187
Pocklington, Peter, 168, 171
Pollock, Sam, 60, 79, 83, 116, 121, 150
Pony Line, 38, *39*
Port Arthur Bearcats, 31
Portland Rosebuds, 14, 17, 19
Potvin, Denis, 117, 141, *148,* 158, *181,* 185
Poulin, Georges, 19
Presse, La (Montreal), 121
Priakin, Sergei, 163
Primeau, Joe, 33, *35*
Production Line, *43,* 44
Pronger, Chris, *273*
Punch Line, 40, *40*
Puttee, Art, 30

Quebec Nordiques, 95, 103, 104, 119, *194,* 203, 204, 208-9, *222, 231, 232, 250, 255* (*See also* Colorado Avalanche)
Quinn, Pat, 176, 178

Ramage, Rob, 103
Raymond, Bertrand, 121
Reagan, Ronald, 219
Reardon, Kenny, 87
Red Army team, 113, 202
Renberg, Mikael, *258*
Renfrew Millionaires (Consentino), *18,* 22

303

Resch, Glenn, 142
Rheaume, Manon, *214, 215, 270*
Ricci, Mike, 209
Richard, Henri (Pocket Rocket), *50, 57, 57, 76, 113, 123, 135*
Richard, Maurice (Rocket), 40, *40,* 43-44, 46, 47, 48, 49, 50, *50,* 51, 54, 56, 57, 58, *59,* 113, 120, *135, 262*
Richard Riot, 58, *59*
Richard Trophy, *262*
Richer, Stephane, *178*
Richter, Mike, *216, 222, 274, 281*
Risebrough, Doug, 119
Rivers, Romeo, 29
Roberts, Jim 119
Robinson, Larry, 113, 116, 119, 121, *137,* 200
Ross, Art, 33, 34
Rousseau, Bobby, 84
Roy, Patrick, 170, 219-220, *219, 231, 275*
Ruel, Claude, 86
Ruotsalainen, Reijo, 176
"Russian Red Wings," 200, *200,* 202
Rutledge, Wayne, 45

Stanley, Lord, of Preston, 10
Saddledome. *See* Canadian Airlines Saddledome
St. Catharines Teepees, 63, 64
St. Louis Blues, 14, 84, 86, *91,* 92, 119, 155, 215, *247, 258, 285*
St. Pats, 31, 32
Sakic, Joe, *203, 232*
Salcer, Ron, 178
Saleski, Don, 110
Salming, Borje, 202
Salo, Tommy, *202*
Samuelsson, Kjell, *190*
Sanderson, Derek, 103
Saskatoon Quakers, 31
Sather, Glen, 119, 138, 151, 157-58, 171, 176, 179
Savard, Denis, 150, 151, *151,* 154
Savard, Serge, 64, 116, 117, 119, 121
Sawchuk, Terry, 30, 40, *65, 71,* 72, 73, *73, 76,* 128

Schmidt, Milt, 34, 36, *38,* 40, 89
Schneider, Mathieu, *236*
Schoenfeld, Jim, 176
Schultz, Dave, 84, 110, 113, *108*
Schultz's Army, 110
Seattle Metropolitans, 20, 26
Seibert, Earl, 25
Selanne, Teemu, 221, *262*
Selke, Frank Sr., 76, 79
Selke Trophy. *See* Frank Selke Trophy
Shanahan, Brendan, *215, 236, 237, 240, 281*
Shanahan, Sean, 116
Sharples, Jeff, 176
Shenkarow, Barry, 204
Shero, Fred, 104, 110
Shore, Eddie, 31, 33-34, *35,* 87
Shutt, Steve, 116, 119
Silver Seven, 13
Simon, Chris, 209
Simpson, Bullet Joe, 31
Simpson, Hack, 29
Sinden, Harry, *97*
Sittler, Darryl, *128*
Skalbania, Nelson, *103*
Spectrum. *See* Philadelphia Spectrum
Skyreach Centre (Edmonton), 205
Smith, Ben, 215
Smith, Billy, 141, *142, 149,* 158, 181, *187, 191*
Smith, Bobby, 172
Smith, Hooley, 28, *28*
Smith, Steve, 165, *166,* 193
Smolinski, Bryan, *216*
Smythe, Conn, 31-32, 33, 35, 37
Smythe, Stafford, 79
Snider, Ed, 112, 163
Soviet Central Red Army team, 113, 202
Soviet Ice Hockey Federation, 163
Spirit of Manitoba Inc., 204
Stanley, Allen, *43*
Stanley, Cup, The (Jenish), 10, 13
Stastny, Peter, 204
Stein, Gil, 210
Stephenson, Wayne, 113

Stewart, Black Jack, 141
Stewart, Gaye, 33
Stewart, Paul, 195
Strachan, Al, 121
Strachan, James, 19
Sudbury Wolves, 31
Summit Series (1972), *94, 95, 96-102, 133*
Sunbelt [teams], American, *168,* 229, 285
Sundin, Mats, *250, 253, 255, 256, 274*
Sunshine League, 121
Suter, Gary, 165
Svoboda, Petr, *241*

Tambellini, Steve, 142
Tampa Bay Lightning, 215
Taylor, Dave, 202, 221
Taylor, Fred (Cyclone), 17, 21-23, *21*
Team Canada, 92, 95, 96-102, 116, 163, 214-15, *267, 270, 271, 273, 275, 276, 279, 281, 287*
Team USA, 161, *162, 163,* 199, 214-15, *216, 271, 274, 276, 281*
Tex's Rangers, 31
(*See also* New York Rangers)
Thomas, Steve, *253*
Thompson, Tiny, 35
Tikhonov, Viktor, 164, 200
Tikkanen, Esa, *187*
Tonelli, John, 150, *152,* 164, *181*
Toronto Granites, 28
Toronto Maple Leafs, 32, *32,* 33, *35,* 36, 38, *39,* 40, *40,* 43, 48, 50, *51,* 54, 58, *61, 65,* 70, 72-73, 76, 78, 79, 82, 84, *87,* 92, 112, 117, *127, 128,* 142, 202, 205, 208, 221, 234, *236,* 250, 253, 255, 256, *291* (*See also* St. Pats)
Torrey, Bill, 141, 142, 149
Trail Smoke Eaters, 31
Tremblay, Jean-Claude, 95, 103
Tremblay, Gilles, 116
Tremblay, Mario, 119
Tretiak, Vladislav, *94,* 95, *97, 101, 102, 106,* 163
Trottier, Brian, 117, 141, *142, 148, 150, 185*

Trudeau, Pierre Elliott, 95

Vachon, Rogatien, 73
Vadnais, Carol, 89, 92
Vadnais, Raymonde, 89
Vaive, Rick, 103
Vanbiesbrouck, John, 219
Vancouver Canucks, 146, 150, 164, 171, 176, 178, 205, 217, *265,* 285
Vancouver Millionaires, 17
Van Impe, Ed, 104, 113
Varsity Grads, 29, 30
Vernon, Mike, *151, 166,* 172
Vezina, Georges, 19-20, *19,* 21
Vezina Trophy, 19, *19,* 87, *133, 160,* 200, 202
Victoria Aristocrats, 17, 24
Victoria Cougars, 24, 25, *25,* 26

Walter, Ryan, 150
Washington Capitals, 14, 150, *258*
Watson, Jim, 104
Watson, Joe, 104
Western Canada Hockey League, 26
Wickenheiser, Doug, 151, 195
Williams, Tiger, *142*
Wilson, Carey, 165
Wilson, Doug, 150
Winnipegs, the, 29
Winnipeg Falcons, 25, 28
Winnipeg Jets, 68, 95, 103, 104, 154, 203, 204-5
Winnipeg Monarchs, 31
Winter, Rich, 178
Worsley, Gump, *45,* 60, 73
Worters, Roy, 23

Yakushev, Alexander, 95
Yashin, Alexei, 221, *260, 262*
Yzerman, Steve, *237, 241, 281*

Zhluktov, Viktor, 163
Ziegler, John, 176, 178, 210-11

Photo Credits

Denis Brodeur Photography: 85; 88 (top and bottom); 90 (top, bottom left and right); 93; 94; 96 (top left and right, bottom left and right); 97 (top and bottom); 98-9; 100; 101 (top, middle, bottom); 102; 106; 107; 114-15; 116; 123; 130; 131; 132; 133 (top and bottom); 134; 135 (top and bottom); 136-7; 284

Graphic Artists/Hockey Hall of Fame: 43 top; 66-7; 69; 71; 74-5; 76; 78; 83; 126; 127; 128; 129; 165.

Hockey Hall of Fame Archives: 2; 10; 11 (bottom); 12; 14; 15; 17; 19; 20; 21; 23; 24; 25; 27; 28; 30 (left and right); 34 (top); 40 (middle and bottom); 44 (top, middle and bottom); 45 (bottom); 47; 54 (top); 68 (bottom); 72 (left and right); 96 (bottom right); 103; 125; 139.

Doug MacLellan/Hockey Hall of Fame: 11 (top); 194

Miles Natal/ Hockey Hall of Fame: 163; 164

Bill Galloway/Hockey Hall of Fame: 13; 18; 46; 49

Imperial Oil – Turofsky/Hockey Hall of Fame: 32; 33; 34 (bottom); 35 (top and bottom); 37; 38 (bottom); 39 (top, bottom, left and right); 40 (top); 41; 42 (top and bottom); 77; 80-1; 82 (top and bottom); 87; 206 (top)

Frank Prazak/Hockey Hall of Fame: 65; 89

Fred Keenan: 91

Bruce Bennett Studios:
Bruce Bennett: 108; 109; 111; 140; 141; 142 (top and bottom); 144-5; 146 (top and bottom); 147; 148; 149; 150; 151; 152 (top and bottom); 153; 154 (left and right); 155; 156; 157; 160; 161; 162; 166 (top); 167; 169; 170; 171; 172-3; 174-5; 178 (top and bottom); 180; 181 (top right, left and bottom right); 182-3; 184 (left, right, bottom right); 185 (left and right); 186 (top and bottom); 187; 188-9; 190 (left); 191; 192; 193 (bottom); 196 (bottom right); 197 (top left and bottom right); 198; 209; 214 (bottom); 216 (bottom); 217 (top left and right, bottom); 219; 222 (right); 226 (top and bottom); 228; 229; 232 (top and bottom); 233 (top left); 234 (left and right); 236 (left and right); 241 (bottom right);

242; 245 (top right); 246 (top and bottom right); 247 (top and bottom); 255; 256; 259 (top); 260; 262 (top and bottom left); 263; 285 (top and bottom left)

S. Wachter: 196 (top)
J. Giamondo: 196 (bottom left); 201; 205; 215; 222 (top left); 224; 230; 231; 238-9; 244; 258; 261
Phil Angers: 197 (top right)
C. Anderson: 199; 236 (bottom); 254
Brian Winkler: 202; 241
Jim McIsaac: 216; 220; 222; (bottom left); 236 (top); 245 (top left and bottom); 259 (bottom); 263 (bottom right);
Bruce Laberge: 219
J. Tremmel: 227
Pichette: 233 (top right); 248-9
H. Dirocco: 233 (bottom)
Vin Pugliese: 246 (bottom left)
Foxall: 240
Leo Redkoles: 253

Canadian Press:
Blaise Edwards: 177

Frank Gunn: 204: 208; 292 (top); 294; 295; 296
Hans Deryk: 210: 212; 268; 269
Jeff McIntosh: 214 top
Denis Paquin: 220: 271: 273 (bottom); 274
Kathie Willens: 272
Kevork Djansezian: 275 (left); 290
Paul Chiasson: 273 (top); 277; 281 (left); 285 (bottom right); 282; 288
Fred Chartrand: 275 (right)
Ryan Ramiorz: 278-9; 283 (right)
Draper: 286-7
Paul Sancya: 291 (bottom)
Chuck Stoody: 287
Jeff Bassett: 289
Bryan Kelsen: 291 (top)
Eric Gay: 291 (top)
Chris Gardner: 292 (bottom)
Keith Srakocic: 293
Donna McWilliam: 297